Walsingham: Pilgrimage and History

Papers presented at the
Centenary Historical Conference
23rd - 27th March 1998

Published by R. C. National Shrine, Walsingham

First Edition in 1999 by the R. C. National Shrine
Pilgrim Bureau, Friday Market,
Walsingham, Norfolk, NR22 6EG.

ISBN 0 9502167 6 3

Printed by
The Lanceni Press Ltd, Fakenham, Norfolk

A Walsingham Centenary Publication

1. Walsingham 100 Years of Pilgrimage 1897 - 1997
(R. C. National Shrine, 1997)

2. Walsingham England's Nazareth by Peter Rollings
(R. C. National Shrine, 1998)

3. Walsingham: Methodism in the 19th Century by John Hawkes
(R. C. National Shrine, 1998)

4. Walsingham: Charlotte Boyd 1837 - 1906 by Kate Moore
(R. C. National Shrine, 1998)

5. Walsingham: Pilgrimage and History
(R. C. National Shrine, 1999)

This book is dedicated to Father Roland Connelly, sm

Priest, Author and Historian

Director of the National Shrine of Our Lady 1968-78

who has done so much to encourage historical studies of

Walsingham and its Shrines.

Foreword

The first pilgrimage to Walsingham in modern times was organised by the Guild of Our Lady of Ransom on 20th August 1897 after the Shrine of Our Lady of Walsingham was restored by rescript of Pope Leo XIII in King's Lynn the previous day.

A year of celebrations and pilgrimage marked the Centenary Year which included a Historical Conferece organised by the National Shrine. Delegates to the Conference came from as far afield as California and Texas and the presence of members of the Anglican, Orthodox, Roman Catholic and other traditions gave our discussions an ecumencial flavour that was wholly appropriate to Walsingham.

The long history of Walsingham is complex and full of pitfalls for the unwary. The speakers to the Conference shared rich fruits borne of detailed study and passionate interest. I am delighted to share their insights to a wider readership.

Rev. A. Williams, sm
Director of the National Shrine

Notes on Contributors

Scilla Landale is a distinguished local historian who started *Guided Tours of Walsingham* in 1988.

Dr. Carole Rawcliffe is Reader and Wellcome Research Fellow in the History of Medicine at the University of East Anglia; she is a former Director of the Centre for East Anglian Studies at the University.

Professor Christopher Harper-Bill is the Director of the Centre of East Anglian Studies at the University of East Anglia.

Rev. Bill McLoughlin, OSM is the Hon. General Secretary of the Ecumenical Society of the Blessed Virgin Mary and joint editor of *Mary is for Everyone, Essays on Mary and Ecumenism* published in 1997. Father McLoughlin has had a long standing interest in the history of Walsingham.

Ethel Hostler was educated at the Universities of London and Cambridge and after a career in teaching and librarianship has made a special study of the life of Charlotte Boyd.

Dom Aidan Bellenger, OSB is a former Headmaster of Downside School and is now the Director of Historical Research at Downside Abbey.

Dr. Paul Richards is the Mayor of King's Lynn and a distinguished authority on the history of the town.

Howard Fears is a resident of Walsingham with a passion for studies in local history which he pursues at the University of East Anglia.

Canon Peter Cobb is the Master of the College of Guardians of the Anglican Shrine of Our Lady of Walsingham. A former Director of Studies at St. Stephen's House, Oxford, he has published widely on liturgy, Church history and the establishment of the Anglican Shrine.

Acknowledgements

I am very grateful to Tim McDonald who as Centenary Co-ordinator worked so hard in planning the Conference and ensuring its success. Anne Milton is our Archivist at the National Shrine and with characteristic thoroughness has proof read all of the papers and is responsible for the choice of many of the illustrations in the book. Debbie Parker has, once again, prepared the manuscript for the printers.

Gerald Stocking gave a wonderfully illustrated talk on the buildings of Walsingham in his uniquely enterataining style; sadly it was not possible to reduce this to the written word for the purposes of this book. However, I am grateful to Dr. Paul Richards who has very kindly allowed us to include a paper on the Red Mount Chapel.

Amonst those who chaired the presentations and discussions were:- Father Martin Warner, the Administrator of the Anglican Shrine; Father Peter Allen, sm, former Director of the National Shrine and Mrs. Janet Marshall, the Education Officer at the Anglican Shrine.

AW

Contents

A PILGRIM'S PROGRESS TO WALSINGHAM

by Scilla Landale, Blue Badge Guide

I would like to start my talk this afternoon by firstly thanking you very much for inviting me to open this Historical Conference - with the eminent lecturers to come, I am delighted that I'm on first!

I would like also to state that the research and production of this talk entitled 'A Pilgrim's Progress to Walsingham' is not viewed from a deeply theological point of view - on such a subject I have no qualifications, others will go into this in greater detail during the week. My approach to the subject is that of a Tour Guide to Walsingham, based hopefully on historical fact!

Before we journey to Walsingham let us first consider briefly - Why Pilgrims and Pilgrimages. The Dictionary's definition is: 'A pilgrim is one who journeys to sacred places as an act of religious devotion; person regarded as journeying to a future life', and so it has always been for all religions: Hindus visit the Ganges, Muslims make their way to Mecca, Buddhists to Sarnath near Benares, and Jews and Christians to Jerusalem and the Holy Land. The basic need in all these pilgrimages is to seek a spiritual advancement by getting as close to the roots of their beliefs as possible. The first Christian pilgrimages were made by the members of the early Christian Church retracing Christ's steps in the Holy Land - particularly Bethlehem and Jerusalem. As the Church spread wider and St. Peter established the Christian Church in the capital of the Roman world in Rome, (where he was subsequently crucified upside down by Emperor Nero in what is now the site of St. Peter's Square), so Rome too became a place of pilgrimage - Christians made the long and hazardous journey to where St. Peter had been martyred.

Pilgrimages to the Holy Land became very difficult during the early Middle Ages, when the area was over run by the 'heathens', and the resulting four Holy Crusades to try and restore the freedom of the Holy Land made any journey extremely hazardous. During these centuries pilgrims looked for Shrines nearer to home and slightly less dangerous to journey to, for example St. James de Compostela in Northern Spain, Canterbury or Walsingham.

This situation helped to establish The Shrine of Our Lady at Walsingham, which ultimately became the premier Shrine to Our Lady in England, known as 'England's Nazareth'.

The early history of the Shrine has been lost in the mists of time, the first account is given by Richard Pynson[1] in his ballad printed in 1496 - plenty of time for embroidering the facts!

In 1061, during the reign of Edward the Confessor, the Lady of the Manor, Richeldis de Faverches, who was a young widow, had a series of visions, or dreams, when the Virgin Mary came to her and showed her the house in Nazareth where the Annunciation took place. The Virgin Mary instructed Richeldis to build a replica of the Holy House here in Walsingham, so that "all that beseech her help, shall find succour there". Richeldis was clearly given, by Our Lady, the dimensions of the little Holy House. The next question was 'where it was to be built'. Richeldis was sure that if she was being instructed to build the Holy House in Walsingham she would be given a sign where to do so.

The following morning, whilst the dew was still on the ground, she came across the River Stiffkey to a field where there were already two holy wells. Near these wells was an area of dry ground the approximate size of the Holy House, surely this was the sign. However life is never that easy, as she walked over the field, she came upon another area of dry ground, the same size as the one by the wells. Richeldis, however, chose the site nearest the wells, and try as the carpenters could to put together the little wooden Holy House, which measured approximately 23 feet 6 inches by 12 feet 10 inches, nothing would fit. Richeldis, feeling very despondent, spent the following night in prayer to Our Lady, and the next day it was discovered that the building had been moved to the other site, some two hundred feet further north east from the wells, and was better constructed than any craftsman of the period could build.

As you can imagine there is an element of doubt over the actual date of this event, with Richard Pynson's Ballad being written some 400 years after the event. So we must allow for a certain amount of latitude! There is a strong feeling among some theologians that the date of 1061 is widely incorrect, and that the event probably took place in the middle of the 12th century but until further firm evidence is discovered the answer will not be known.

What happened after the replica of the Holy House had been moved and built at Walsingham? Richeldis seems to fade out of the picture. The ballad says that Our Lady showed many miracles "too numerous to mention" to all those to who came to see Her, perhaps Richeldis employed a priest to look after the Holy House, we do not know.

By the middle of the 12th century we come onto firmer historical fact. Geoffrey de Faverches, Richeldis' son, is going away on the second Crusade (1145-1149), before he leaves England, he makes a Charter[2] "granting to God and St. Mary and to Edwin, his chaplain, in perpetuity The Chapel which my mother has founded in Walsingham in honour of Mary ever Virgin, together with possession of the Church of All Saints of the same village, and all its appurtenances in lands, tithes, and rents, to come in to the possession of Edwyn on the day on which I leave for Jerusalem". Edwyn, Geoffrey's Chaplain, was responsible for bringing the Augustinian Canons to Walsingham in 1153, the first Prior, Ralph, governed from 1153 to 1173. Geoffrey's actual gift was finally confirmed by Bishop William Turbus, Bishop of Norwich in 1169. The Patrons were Robert de Brucurt and Roger, Earl of Clare, who also gave the Priory "a mill in the said town of Walsingham, together with the rights of milling usually reserved for landlords." The de Clare family remained Patrons and overall Lords of the Manor for centuries. It is interesting to note that the Walsingham Chapel of Our Lady must have been of some importance before 1153, as Geoffrey made over the Chapel plus its possessions of tithes, lands and indeed the Parish Church to be cared for by a religious order.

Why the Augustinian Canons were invited to establish the Priory at Walsingham rather than, say, the Benedictines is not known. The Canons followed the Rule of St. Augustine of Hippo: the Order reached England in 1104, the first Priory being St. Boltoph's at Colchester. Their Rule was less strict than the Benedictine's, the Canons were ordained priests. They were able to work outside the cloister caring for the sick, helping with almshouses, etc. They were medicant, a healing Order, so maybe with the pilgrims already coming to the Chapel of Our Lady to seek succour, it was felt that the followers of the Rule of St. Augustine were better qualified to run the Priory. Alternatively, the Augustinian Order was the latest religious order to arrive in England, and was perhaps seen as very modern and popular! The Augustinian Canons were also called 'Black Canons' from their dress - a long black robe and a black hat.

Very little remains of the early Priory buildings: the Norman Arch now marking the entrance to the twin wells and bath is one of the earliest. As well as this being the site of the first attempt to build the Holy House, there was a Chapel here dedicated to St. Laurence, in which was kept a Relic of St. Peter's Finger[3] - of colossal size according to Erasmus.

Roman Catholic Pilgrimage from Oscott and Douai, Easter 1936, at the Wells in the Priory Grounds.

The fortunes of the Priory improved; by the increasing popularity in the cult and following of Our Lady, that is Marian Devotion; the difficulties of pilgrimage to the Holy Land; and the growing awareness that something miraculous had taken place in Walsingham - pilgrims coming to the Holy House and drinking the water from the wells, claimed that their prayers were being answered. For example, in the early 14th century, one Thomas Gatele[4] who later became Sub-Prior, "in his boyhood was submerged in the Well of the Blessed Virgin Mary and died, but by a miracle of the Blessed Virgin Mary was restored to life."

By 1226 news of the happenings at Walsingham had reached the ears of King Henry III[5], and he was to become the first of many Royal visitors. On the 3rd and 4th April 1226 Henry III visited Walsingham, when he granted the

Canons the right to hold a weekly market, plus a two day fair over the Feast of the Holy Cross. Henry III made about 13 visits to Walsingham, and there is no doubt that Walsingham's rise to national fame was due more to his support than to anyone else. He gave the Canons the 'Royal Seal of Approval'. In 1232 he gave the Canons 40 great oaks for the work on the Church, and in 1234 a further 20 oaks were given 'to make a certain building' these timbers came from his forests near Newcastle upon Tyne and Colchester, probably transported to Walsingham by sea. As well as timber he gave large gifts of wax and tapers to be offered at the Chapel of St. Mary, a gold crown and vestments to be placed on the image of St. Mary, and the Canons, the right to hold other fair days.

As the popularity of the Priory increased, so it became necessary to enlarge the Priory Church to cater for the pilgrims visiting the Chapel of Our Lady. It appears that this took place in the middle of the 14th century, instigated by the then Prior, Prior John Snoring. In 1384 Prior Snoring[6] was dismissed as Prior by the other Canons, because they felt he was wasting the revenues of the Priory, presumably because of the ambitious expansion of the Church: it was claimed he was interfering with the arrangements for the weekly market: and perhaps worse, Prior Snoring was trying to raise the status of the Priory to that of an Abbey - whereby his status would be enhanced to that of Abbot. John Snoring was given leave to plead his case in Rome, but he was not reinstated. We do however have him to thank for the magnificent East Window which still stands today.

Before its Dissolution in 1538 The Augustinian Priory to the Blessed Virgin Mary must have been an impressive establishment. We know the Church was 250 feet in length, built of Barnack Stone, Clipsham Limestone and flint. The footings remain of the West Tower, the Central Tower we know had four gilded spires. Philip, Earl of Arundel,[7] wrote a wonderful ballad when he was a prisoner in the Tower of London, having fallen from grace from Queen Elizabeth I:

> Levell, levell with the ground,
> the Towers doe lye,
> Which with their golden glittering tops,
> Pearsed onto the skye.

The towers would have been visible from a great distance. The East Window would have had the High Altar set in front of it.

As well as increasing the church, Prior Snoring also had the Holy House, which was made of wood, encased in a larger Chapel. The chronicler, William of Worcester[8] wrote an account of the 'Novum Opus' (the new work) when he toured Norfolk in 1479. By encasing the Shrine in a larger chapel, it enabled the pilgrims to enter the Holy House from the nave of the Priory Church, and leave through a door on the far side, so keeping a free moving flow of pilgrims. The finishing touches to the building work of the new Chapel must have been rather slow, when King Henry VIII visited Walsingham in 1511 the windows of the new Chapel had not been glazed, and Henry made two payments amounting to £43 11s.4d. to his glazier Barnard Flower[9] to glaze the windows of the Lady Chapel, as a thank-you offering for the birth of Prince Henry. Barnard Flower is famous for his work at King's College Chapel, Cambridge.

The Dutch Humanist, Erasmus,[10] whilst studying in Cambridge, visited Walsingham in 1514, and left a very vivid account of the Holy House "If you look in you will say it is a seat for Gods, so bright and shiny is it all over with jewels, gold and silver". He describes how pilgrims came up steps from the Priory Church into the Holy House, which was very dark inside except for the fantastic blaze of light caused by all the votive candles burning, and the Statue of Our Lady with Christ on her lap covered with jewels, brooches, rings, crowns, etc. and lovely raiment all given by grateful pilgrims. Standing near the door to the Chapel of Our Lady stood an Augustinian Canon collecting the gifts and tokens from the pilgrims - Erasmus gave them the prayer which is still used today, although he was doubtful whether the Canons would be able to read his verses!

In his Colloquy '*Pilgrimage for Religions Sake*' (Peregrinoatio Religionis Ergo) Erasmus's character, Menedemus, asks his friend Ogygius why he visited Walsingham, to which he replies "Nothing new; only those usual petitions, the health of my family, the increase of my estate, a long and happy life in this world, and eternal happiness in the next." Surely the sentiments of the majority of pilgrims visiting Walsingham in both Medieval times and today.

In later writings Erasmus was rather derogatory over the authenticity of the relics held at Walsingham. As well as having a relic of St. Peter's finger in the Chapel of St. Laurence, the main relic was the Phial of 'Virgin's Milk' or the chalk from the cave in which the Holy Family stayed during their flight to Egypt. According to Erasmus, through Ogyguis, in his Colloquy 'Pilgrimage for Religions Sake', the inscription on how the relic reached Walsingham was fixed high above the High Altar in the Priory Church. What happened to these Relics after the Priory was dissolved in 1538 there is no record.

Erasmus also described the village of Walsingham as "living by scarcely anything else but the concourse of pilgrims". And so it did, the whole village was planned to provide accommodation for visiting pilgrims. The centre of the village moved away from the Parish Church across the River Stiffkey and was established round the Priory.

In 1431 we know that there were at least 20 hostelries in the village, because during Easter of that year four of them were burnt down by disgruntled pilgrims who thought they were being overcharged. Today Walsingham is a fine example of a planned Medieval village with some excellent examples of timber-framing, and indeed the majority of them are today providing accommodation for pilgrims.

The Friary was established by Elizabeth, Countess de Burgh, in 1347.[11] It is situated on the edge of the village being built just before The Black Death, in 1348/49 which swept through England and reduced the population by a half to two-thirds, resulted in fewer pilgrims coming to Walsingham, and therefore there was no need for the village to keep expanding as originally planned around the Friary.

King Edward III was a frequent visitor to Walsingham. He endorsed the arrival of the Friars, which was met with great opposition from Canons, who appealed against the establishment of the Friary thinking that they would 'hi-jack' the pilgrims before they reached the Shrine and relieve them of any 'gifts' they might have. Edward III granted the Friars the right to hold a market in the Friday Market Place. The dues from the stallholders in Friday Market went to the Friary, the stallholders in the Common Place - Tuesday Market Place - went to the Priory! The Black Lion Hotel, is named after his Queen, Philippa Hainault, who had the black lion on her coat of arms.

Having described the founding of the Shrine and the building of the Priory and Church, let us now consider the pilgrims who visited the Shrine and the pilgrim routes. I mentioned earlier that initially the basic need in all pilgrimages was to seek a spiritual advancement by getting as close as possible to the roots of Christian belief by following the footsteps of Christ and his Disciples.

By the Middle Ages reasons for going on pilgrimage had became more complicated and demanding. The average life span was quite short, and death through plague, illness, poverty, childbirth and wars was very real.

By the 14th century one of the main reasons for visiting Shrines or a Holy Relic was to save one's soul. The great fear in the Medieval period was what will happen after death, the after life was divided into three sections - Heaven, Hell and Purgatory. Purgatory was a man-made doctrine, it does not appear in the bible, but the fear of dying and going to Hell or spending years 'floating about in Purgatory' was very real.

Pilgrims would go on pilgrimage to 'save their souls', or upon their death send somebody to a Holy Shrine to 'say masses for their souls'. For example, in 1536 Katherine of Aragon's Will[12] provided 'that some personages go to Our Lady of Walsingham on pilgrimage and distribute 20 nobles on the way'. (A noble was worth 6s. 8d.). Going on pilgrimage to a Holy Shrine was also a way of atoning for one's sins, an effort of winning favour with God. Some Shrines used to sell indulgences, that is repentance to sinners if they paid enough. Indulgences were meant to shorten the time spent in Purgatory by the penitent.

A pilgrimage, which was often very hazardous and dangerous, could also be ordered as a penance for a crime, rather than another form of punishment. It didn't always work as we see from 1364, when one Philip Crikyere[13] who should have been in Hertford Jail for extortion, managed to secured his Keeper's licence to go on pilgrimage to Walsingham. Unfortunately on his way back, Philip got involved in a brawl in which he killed a man!

Another very important reason for going on pilgrimage to a Shrine or to touch a Holy Relic was the cure of the sick. We have an excellent illustration of this in The Paston Letters,[14] which are a wonderful insight into life in 15th century England. On 28th September 1443, Margaret Paston wrote from Oxnead to her husband John who was away at the Inner Temple, London, and obviously not well "and I thank you for the letter that you sent me, for by my troth, my mother and I were not at ease from the time that we knew of your sickness till we knew verily of your mending. My mother promised another image of wax of the weight of yourself to Our Lady of Walsingham and to St. Leonard's Priory, Norwich". Similarly in September 1517, Cardinal Wolsey[15] visited the Shrine to Our Lady in Walsingham to "fulfil a vow and also to take air and exercise which may correct the weakness of his stomach."

Pilgrims also came to Walsingham to thank Our Lady for answering their prayers in time of great trial or need, as well as for seeking her help in advance. We have some good illustrations of this:

Edward I's attachment to Walsingham was of long standing, probably instilled in him by his Father, Henry III, the first Royal Patron of the Shrine. We are told by a reliable chronicler that on one occasion during his youth, Edward[16] was playing chess in a vaulted room when he suddenly had the urge to move away from his seat, immediately a large stone fell from the roof onto the spot where he had been sitting. Because of which miracle he ever afterwards most ardently honoured Our Lady of Walsingham. Indeed he visited Walsingham no less than 14 times during his reign.

Another great devotee of Walsingham was King Henry VII. When his throne was under threat from imposters, Perkin Warbeck and Lambert Simnel, he made pilgrimage to Walsingham in April 1487 where 'he prayed devoutly before the image of the Blessed Virgin Mary that he might be preserved from the wiles of his enemies.' After the defeat of Lambert Simnel at the Battle of Stoke in 1487, Henry VII sent Christopher Urswick to Walsingham with the military standard which he had used against the enemy who he had defeated "to offer thanks for the victory in the Shrine of the Blessed Virgin, and to place the standard there as a memorial of the favour he had received from God."[17]

In 1511 Sir Edward Howard wrote a letter to Henry VIII in which he states that he has given Master Arthur Plantagenant, liberty to go Walsingham on landing after naval action off Brest "for Sir when he was in extreme danger and hope gone from him he called upon Our Lady of Walsingham for help and comfort and made a vow that, if it please God and Her to deliver him out of that peril, he would never eat flesh nor fish until he had seen her. Sir, I assure you that he was in marvellous danger, for it was a marvel that the ship being under all her sails striking a rock with her stern did not break upon into pieces at the first stroke".[18]

THE PILGRIM

Very little information is available about the ordinary pilgrim. The only people whose movements were regularly recorded in Medieval times were those of the Kings of England, who in the matter of pilgrimages may or may not have resembled their subjects. One exception to this is, of course, Margery Kempe[19] of King's Lynn whose writings give wonderful accounts of her pilgrimages to the Holy Land, Rome and briefly in 1433 to Walsingham. She may have made other visits to Walsingham but these are not recorded, maybe a visit to Walsingham was too local to be really worth mentioning.

When setting out on pilgrimage the pilgrim had to prepare himself for his journey as follows: "The pilgrim should prepare himself to pardon the injuries done to him, to restore everything belonging to others, and live according to the law, because without this first and necessary disposition every hope and every fatigue is in vain." Margery Kempe, like all married women going on pilgrimage, had to seek permission from her husband as well as her local parson.

Before finally leaving for their pilgrimage, pilgrims would attend a Church service, to make their final confessions, and be presented with the pilgrim tokens - the pilgrim staff, rosary, scrip. The really devout Pilgrims wore a long grey gown, made of the cheapest material, which in some cases had a cross on it: they wore a broad rimmed hat, which often had crosses or the scallop shell of St. James de Compostela sown around the brim: they carried a rosary and a scrip or small bag which contained their slender provisions, holy water, and a staff or stick. On their hat and coats they pinned the pilgrim badges or palm leaves which they had collected on their travels. Looking at various medieval illustrations, particularly those concerned with Chaucer's *Canterbury Tales* I don't think all pilgrims bothered with such extreme forms of dress.

THE ROADS

The roads, known as the King's Highway, were full of potholes and extremely uneven. In theory the land-owners had to maintain their surface and clear the land to within 200 feet of either side of the road to deter robbers. In many cases it was seen as the role of the religious houses to maintain the roads. By the 15th century roads were thronged with travellers of all sorts - messengers bringing writs and letters from the King and from the departments of state to sheriffs and other local officials. Sheriff's messengers making returns to London; lawyers, litigants, judges and juries journeying to the courts. Merchants and their servants carting their goods to markets, fairs and ports. Farmers driving cattle and sheep. Nobles and their retinues with carts loaded with furnishings moving from one house to another or on their way to court or to parliament. Pilgrims and friars on religious business, peddlars and itinerant workmen, minstrels and entertainers, and all too often vagabonds and robbers. Pilgrims were encouraged to travel in groups meeting together at roadside crosses. There were few taverns and hostelries outside the towns, the main places providing rest and refreshment were religious houses. One Walsingham Ballad puts this very well:

> Gentle heardsman tell me
> Of curtesy I thee pray,
> Unto the towne of Walsingham
> Which is the right and ready way?
>
> Unto the town of Walsingham,
> The Way is hard for to be gon,
> And very crooked are those pathes
> For you to find out all alone.[20]

The star galaxy - The Milky Way was called The Walsingham Way because it seemed to direct pilgrims to Walsingham!

THE PILGRIM ROUTE FROM LONDON

Geoffrey Chaucer in *The Canterbury Tales* puts the Tabard Inn in Southwark well and truly on the map for pilgrims travelling to Canterbury. For pilgrims preparing to travel to Walsingham there appear to have been one or two inns in the Holborn area where they forgathered. The Chequers and The Bell Inns in Holborn were where the carriers of Walsingham lodged. The carrier arrived every second Thursday, it also appears that the Footposte (an early form of postal service) from Walsingham came to the Crosskeys in Holborn.[21]

First Student Cross Pilgrimage to Walsingham leaving London, Easter 1948.

From Holborn, pilgrims left London by various routes - Islington, Aldgate and Bethnal Green to Shoreditch, Tottenham, Edmonton to Waltham Cross. From Waltham Cross and Waltham Abbey the pilgrims went via Cheshunt, Hoddesdon, Ware, Puckeridge, Barkway, to Whittlesford - where the wayside Chapel at Duxford is still visible. From Whittlesford the route went to Babraham and then to Newmarket - so called because in 1226 the town of Exning was burnt down, and as a result a New Market (Novum Mercatum)[22] was built and traffic diverted through it. Horses are mentioned at an early stage: in 1453 Queen Margaret of Anjou, wife of Henry VI, paid £13 6s. 8d. to two men whose stables were burnt down.

From Newmarket the pilgrim could either branch off and visit the Shrine of St. Edmund at Bury St. Edmunds, or continue North to cross into Norfolk by the Ferry at Brandon. King Henry VI made three pilgrimages to Walsingham and in each case he varied his pilgrim route.

Having crossed into Norfolk at Brandon Ferry, the route went via Weeting, Bromeholme, Ickburgh - where there was a Chapel dedicated to Our Lady and St. Lawrence - to Hillborough. Here, the ruins of the Wayside Chapel dedicated to 'St. Margaret of Antioch' which was founded by 1207, are still just visible - a pile of ivy growing over a heap of stones. From Hillborough the pilgrims went to The Priory of Great Cressingham, and to North and South Pickenham. In a letter to King Henry VIII written by Charles Brandon, Duke of Suffolk from Castle Rising dated 17th March 1517, he stated that he met Queen Katherine of Aragon on Friday 13th at "Pykenhem Wade" on her way to Walsingham and escorted her the rest of the journey.[23]

Castle Acre Priory may well have been another stopping off point for pilgrims. This Cluniac Priory had a relic of St. Philip's arm,[24] and its large infirmary indicates that it was used extensively by pilgrims, many of whom may have been too sick to continue on their pilgrimage. Leaving Castle Acre the route went to Great Dunham, Litcham - where there used to be a Pilgrim's Chapel and a Hermitage at Tittleshall - and on to Hempton.

The Augustinian Priory of St. Stephen's, Hempton was situated at the end of a dam or causeway connecting Hempton and Fakenham.[25] A mill nearby was rented off the Priory of Castle Acre for an annual payment of 42 shillings. Over this millpool ran a bridge, known as the Bridgemill, which carried the high road to Walsingham. Both bridge and causeway needed yearly repair because of the flooding of the River Wensum. There was a great row between the men of Fakenham, Hempton Priory and Castle Acre. The Fakenham men wanted the pilgrim route to run through Fakenham, and accused the Priory of not keeping up the bridges and causeway resulting in the Priory being fined by the Sheriff's Court in 1364. In 1461 the Prior of Castle Acre reduced the annual rent on the water mill from 42 to 20 shillings. From Hempton the route went to Barsham, the Slipper Chapel and Walsingham.

THE ROUTE FROM NORWICH

The Priors of Walsingham, like other Norfolk people of importance, had a house in Norwich, this stood near the West end of St. George's Church, Colegate. Norwich was a pilgrimage centre for pilgrims visiting Dame Julian of Norwich, or passing through on their way to view the Relic of the Holy Cross at Bromholm or to Walsingham. The Great Hospital, founded in 1249 by Bishop Walter de Suffield, hosted large numbers of pilgrims.

In June 1469 King Edward IV and his brother Richard, Duke of Gloucester, came on pilgrimage to Walsingham from Norwich.[26] They left Norwich through St. Augustine's or Coslany Gate and rode to Drayton and Hellesdon. The River Wensum was crossed at Attlebridge, beside a Chapel dedicated to Our Lady maintained by a hermit called Thomas.[27]

The road went to Lenwade, Sparham and onto Bawdeswell, where according to Chaucer

> The Reeve was old and choleric and thin,
> His beard was shaven closely to the skin,
> ....he came, as I heard tell,
> From Norfolk, near a place called Baldeswell.[28]

Bintree, the next place on the route, is interestingly enough, the site of the earliest recorded mention of a commoner coming on pilgrimage to Walsingham. In 1261 John le Chaumpeneys[29] and his mother were on pilgrimage to Walsingham when they put up at a hostelry in Bintree owned by Roger le Worth. It appears that a dispute arose between the host, Roger le Worth, and some of the other guests. In the fracas that followed, John le Chaumpeneys, with others, was set upon and so kicked and wounded by the host that he scarcely escaped with his life. In trying to escape, John le Chaumpeneys hit back at his host with a stick with fatal result. The King in answer to the petition of the same le Chaumpeneys commissioned John de Cave, constable, to set up an inquiry into the matter, and to ascertain by oath of honest and liege men of Norfolk, whether the killing was in self-defence or whether it was otherwise. The Sheriff of Norfolk is ordered to summon such a jury before him, this was dated The Tower of London, 15th February 1261. There is no record of the final verdict, and it is only because of this incident that we actually have a record of a 'commoner' going on pilgrimage.

PILGRIMS COMING FROM THE WEST

Pilgrims journeying to Walsingham from the north and west of England, or coming by sea from Europe all had to pass through King's Lynn. The journey across the 14 mile stretch of sand between Holbeach on the Lincolnshire side to Walpole Cross Keys on the Norfolk side of the Wash was extremely treacherous, and could not be attempted without a guide. In many cases travellers from the north journeyed further south to Crowland before turning east. Three main routes converged on Crowland - from the north through Spalding, the west from Stamford and the south from Peterborough.

On 30th June 1519 the Gatekeeper of Crowland Abbey was reported to the Bishop of Lincoln for amongst other misdeeds, when pilgrims came to the Abbey Gate asking directions to Walsingham he would only laugh at them, or direct them wrongly out of sheer malice ![30] From Crowland pilgrims could travel to Wisbech via the ferry across the Nene at Guyhirn, then up to King's Lynn, or through to Swaffham and up via Castle Acre to Walsingham.

Pilgrims came in vast numbers by sea from the north of England, and from Europe. King's Lynn was the fourth largest Medieval port and a member of the Hanseatic Trading League. Pilgrims as well as merchant goods, travelled back and forth from the Low Countries, France, Germany and Scandinavia. Licences were issued to ship owners to convey pilgrims to various ports around England.

Between February 1354 and April 1357, when England was at war with France, Edward III banned all pilgrims leaving England, and ordered that all incomers were to be searched. In 1399, the King authorised the payment of £9 to John, Duke of Brittany, for his expenses in going to and returning from Walsingham. Similarly a licence was issued to the Duke of Anjou to visit the Shrines of St. Thomas of Canterbury and Our Lady at Walsingham. The Scots were also given licence to pilgrimage to Walsingham. In 1364, David Bruce was given safe conduct by the King to make a pilgrimage to Walsingham.[31]

In 1349, it appears that there was some assistance to ships coming into King's Lynn, in that it is reported that John Puttock erected a 100 foot high cross at the entrance to the Crouch near the sea shore as a guidance to mariners.[32] The map of Lynn Haven and the River Ouse dated 1791 shows The Crouch, running north of Lynn going out into the Wash. The records show that William Bateman, Bishop of Norwich, 1344-55, was approached by the Mayor and Commonality of Lynn with a petition that he, the Bishop, admit John Puttock as a hermit to dwell in a cave on the shore which he had made, until he could build himself a proper dwelling.

PILGRIM BADGES

Pilgrims getting on and off the ships have inadvertently left a wealth of treasure behind them, in the form of pilgrim badges. These lead or pewter badges were made by the Canons in Walsingham in vast quantities during the 14th to 16th centuries, for sale as souvenirs to pilgrims visiting the Shrine.

When the King's Commissioners, Richard Southwell, Thomas le Strange and Mr. Hoges, came to dissolve The Priory at Walsingham in August 1538, they tried to justify their actions by claiming that the Canons were counterfeiting money.[33] It was claimed that they found a secret place in the house, where no Canon entered, and when they did gain entry they found instruments, pots, bellows, phials of such colours - gold and silver - "nothing wanting that should belong to the arte of multyplyeng."

It was most likely that the Canons were making pilgrim badges such as the badges of the Annunciation, the Statue of Our Lady, or indeed illustrating the miracle of the Knight's Gate. In 1314, a Knight called Sir Ralph Boutetout was fleeing from his enemies; after praying to Our Lady for help, he found that he had miraculously passed through a little wicket gate into the safety of the Priory Grounds, whilst still mounted on his horse, and was thus saved.[34]

Pilgrims going from Shrine to Shrine would make collections of these badges together with small pewter ampullae for holding Holy Water. Over the years many pilgrim badges fell off the hats and coats of the pilgrims as they boarded ship. The collection in King's Lynn was started in the 19th century by Thomas Pung, a King's Lynn Jeweller. He discovered the little badges in the Purfleet, and paid local children to search for them in the mud.

THE RED MOUNT CHAPEL

King's Lynn was richly endowed with five separate religious houses presumably providing for the welfare of pilgrims, but the most intriguing and least known about is The Red Mount Chapel.

The Red Mount Chapel.

Did pilgrims arriving in Bishop's (King's) Lynn by either boat or overland visit Our Lady of the Mount - or The Red Mount Chapel which is perhaps the best or most complete example of a pilgrims wayside Chapel in this country? There appears at present to be no firm answer as to the role played by this unique Chapel in the life of Medieval pilgrims. However for want of historical fact, we shall assume that pilgrims came to the Red Mount in their hundreds to thank Our Lady for their safe journey across the sea or overland, and for guidance for their continued pilgrimage to Walsingham and beyond.

Was the original building of The Red Mount a small fortress built outside The Town Walls but within the wet foss? The Chapel stands on a small artificial hill about 12 feet high with the Gaunock stream behind and the ruins of Gaunock Gate to the west. In 1469 Edward IV came to Lynn with great retinue and was lodged in the Red Mount.[35] It must, therefore, have been well fortified as the King was retreating from Warwick and would not have lodged in a place without fortification. Maybe originally the Red Mount was much larger?

The Chapel[36] consists of three stories. The Lower Chapel (bassa ecclesia) is a high barrel-vaulted room and is the oldest part of the building. Some of the brickwork in the walls probably dates from 1320, when the first mention is made of the chapel and corresponds with the stonework of the town's defences of this period. This chapel now appears to be about 12 feet underground, although originally it had a doorway leading to the outside. The chapel is now completely empty but there are various recesses in the walls which would either have held water stoups, lamps or statues. The largest recess, sometimes referred to as 'The Holy Sepulchre' is on the south wall and this may perhaps have held an altar. This chamber can only be entered by one of the two staircases which are built into the walls surrounding the three chambers of the building. The stairs from the lower chapel lead up to the East Door which was probably used by the priests.

The Middle Chamber is very small, and was probably the vestry. In this priests' cell there are two deep recesses in the walls, a niche for a lamp and hole to carry off the smoke - as in the chapel below. There are signs that other passages lead out of this chamber but these have been blocked up.

The Upper Chapel is quite different from the rest of the building, and was added later in the early 16th century - could this be the work of John Westell who was responsible for some of the work at King's College, Cambridge, and employed by the Bishop of Lincoln? This is a little gem of architectural design. It is a miniature Church being in the form of a cross measuring from east to west 17 feet and north to south 14 feet.

It is a unique example of late perpendicular architecture, with an extremely rich groined roof, with fan tracery springing from four slender columns at the corners. This design in Ketton Stone is very similar to King's College, Cambridge. The Chapel receives its light through quatrefoil windows at the cardinal points. In two of the walls are niches for saints and a holy water stoup and a recess for lamps. The walls of the upper chapel are pierced with square openings filled with elaborate tracery so that worshippers outside on the stairs could see and hear the service being conducted inside the Chapel. Access into and out of the Chapel is by a double staircase leading up to and out of the Upper Chapel, this allowed for a free flow of pilgrims passing through the Chapel.

One of the earliest mentions of the Red Mount is the establishment in 1329 of the Guild of St. Fabian and Sebastian, whose brethren met on 23rd January each year at The Red Mount to "sing an anthem to Our Ladye" and make an offering at her shrine or forfeit half a pound of wax. In 1480 William March left the sum of 6s. 8d. to the fabric of the chapel of St. Mary the Virgin upon Guanock Hill. In the same year William Spink, Prior of Lenne, commissioned an oratory to accommodate the multitudes of pilgrims wending their way through Lynn to Walsingham. He chose the site of the Red Mount, which was just outside the boundary of the Lynn Borough. The Lynn Corporation Hall Books record that without receiving the necessary permission of the Corporation, the Prior of Lynn had commenced to build a chapel on the Red Mount site. The Town Chamberlain promptly informed the Prior that no building could be erected on common land without the authorisation of the Corporation - the building work was stopped. In June 1483 the Corporation approved the Prior's intention and appointed a small committee, lead by Mayor Thomas Thoresby to interview and "commune with the Prior for the ground of the hill called The Ladye of the Mount for the wele of the Commons." In January 1484 Robert Currance was granted a licence to build the chapel provided he gave satisfactory sureties that the people would not be deprived of their grazing rights!

The Prior of Lynn who instigated the building of the Chapel as a wayside oratory for the pilgrims, received considerable income from the Chapel. For example during the first year of Henry VIII's reign the offerings at the Chapel were £16 10s., compared with offerings at St. Nicholas Chapel of £6 4s. and St. James's of £2 6s. 9d.[37] In 1498 Henry VII gave 3s. 4d. to the Altar of Our Lady of the Mount, and other gifts amounting to 13s. 4d.

Although probably used as a wayside Chapel for pilgrims coming to Walsingham for a comparatively short time, the enigma of the history and structure of the Red Mount Chapel has fascinated historians and theologians for centuries!

Centenary Mass 19th August 1997, The Walks, King's Lynn. The Red Mount Chapel to the left.

Continuing east from King's Lynn, pilgrims left Lynn by the East Gate, which was demolished in 1800, through Gaywood and onto Witton, or Wootton Gap. When Henry VII visited Lynn from Walsingham he was met by the Mayor at Witton Gap.

From here the pilgrim could either turn north and go through Castle Rising and then to Docking, Stanhoe, North Creake and Walsingham, or due east via Hillington where the bases of four pilgrim crosses are still visible, but these are not original. Flitcham Priory was dedicated to The Blessed Virgin Mary and was a cell to Walsingham Priory, in 1370 there were six canons in residence. Coxford Priory was also dedicated to The Blessed Virgin Mary and run by the Augustinian Canons. It had many benefactors, and as early as 1291 it received rents from 42 parishes, and in 1534 was valued about £122. However, it too was not without its faults, in 1281 the Canons were reported to "be chatting up the girls, and hunting too much!" Edward I stayed at Coxford Priory on the occasion of his pilgrimage to Walsingham in 1277.[38]

From Coxford the route went through Dunton, Sculthorpe, to East Barsham. East Barsham Manor built in 1484, was a stopping off point for Henry VIII when he came on pilgrimage to Walsingham in 1511. It is said that he walked the last two miles into Walsingham in bare feet. Close to the present house stood a Chapel dedicated to St. Saviour of The Greeting (The Annunciation) of Our Lady.[39]

The last Wayside Chapel visited by pilgrims to Walsingham was at Houghton St. Giles. Dedicated to St. Catherine of Alexandra, it is known today as the Slipper Chapel. The Knights of St. Catherine once guarded the road to Nazareth and the Holy House. Built in the mid 14th century, the Slipper Chapel is a perfect example of the 'Decorated Period' of architecture. Here the pilgrims prepared themselves, both spiritually and physically, for the end of their long and painful pilgrimage. Its name, the Slipper Chapel, could have two meanings; it is thought that pilgrims walked the last mile and a quarter of their pilgrimage barefoot from the Chapel to The Shrine in Walsingham; the other meaning could be that it was called the slype Chapel, a slype being a passage way between the inner and outer cloister in a priory - thus marking the last chapel and passage way before the great Shrine of Our Lady.

THE DISSOLUTION OF THE SHRINE OF THE SHRINE OF OUR LADY OF WALSINGHAM

To go into the why's and wherefores of Henry VIII's Dissolution of the Monasteries would take too long. I will just say that the two major contributing factors which resulted in such drastic action were firstly the Pope's refusal to annul Henry VIII's marriage to Queen Katherine of Aragon, and secondly the extreme wealth of the monasteries, which Henry coveted to help pay for building up his navy and defences on the south coast to counter any possible attack on England by Catholic Europe. The whole matter was more than ably handled by his Vicar General, Thomas Cromwell, Earl of Essex.

In 1534 Cromwell ordered an inventory to be taken of all the monasteries in England. This was known as the Valor Ecclesiasticus. The value put on Walsingham showed it to be the richest Priory in Norfolk after Norwich Cathedral, with a gross general income estimated at £707 7s. 10d. and a net value of £652 4s. 11d.[40]

In 1534 the Prior, Richard Vowell, and 21 other Canons were amongst the first Augustinian Canons to sign the Act of Supremacy, acknowledging

Henry VIII as Supreme Head of the Church in England.[41] Richard Vowell did all he could to try and save the Priory from total destruction, there was local opposition to the closures.

In May 1537, 12 local men were implicated in a plot opposed not only to the closure of the monasteries, but also their concern as to their livelihoods if the Shrine at Walsingham was closed, their objections to the taxes being charged, the enclosure of common land, and their wish to support their colleagues in Yorkshire who had joined The Pilgrimage of Grace. News of which had arrived at Lynn via some Cornish soldiers who came from the north on pilgrimage to Walsingham. By the time the Norfolk plot was discovered the Northern Rising had been put down. As a result of the Walsingham Conspiracy, Thomas Cromwell had the 11 conspirators put to death - five in Norwich, two in Great Yarmouth, William Guisborough and John Peacock in King's Lynn,[42] and Nicholas Mileham, the sub-prior, and George Guisborough were brought back to Walsingham and hung, drawn and quartered on a field just outside Walsingham, which is still called The Martyr's Field, on 30th May 1537.

The popularity of the Shrine continued right up to its Dissolution on the 4th August 1538. Following a Royal Injunction in 1538 "Forbidding the Placing of Candles before images and other superstitious practices," the statue of Our Lady of Walsingham was taken up to Chelsea in London and burnt. The occasion was chronicled in July 1538 by Charles Wriothesley, the Windsor Herald, who wrote a chronicle of England during the reigns of The Tudors. He recorded that "The images of Our Ladye of Walsingham and Ipswich were brought up to London with all the jewels that hung about them at the King's Commandment, and divers other images both in England and Wales, that were used for common pilgrimages, because people should use no more idolatry unto them, and they were burnt at Chelsea by my Lord Privy Seal - Cromwell."

On 4th August 1538, the Priory of the Annunciation of the Blessed Virgin Mary was dissolved. The Canons were turned away with pensions, and Prior Richard Vowell was given the 'living' of North Creake. The Priory[43] was torn down, and the windows, doors, stone called free stone, glass, iron, slates and tiles, were sold off in lots for a total of £55 15s. 11d. The following year the site was sold to Sir Thomas Sydney, governor of the Lazar House, for £90.[44] The Franciscan Friary was also surrendered in 1538 to the Bishop of Dover, it was only valued at £3![45]

As he died, it is said that Henry VIII had a vision of the monks coming to send his soul to Hell.

THE MODERN PILGRIMAGE REVIVAL

Today Walsingham is once again a thriving Pilgrimage Village, the wheel of history has almost come full circle. After centuries of little pilgrim activity to Walsingham, the site of the Priory fell into ruins.

The modern revival of Walsingham as a place of pilgrimage is another talk in its own right, but to put it very briefly and simplistically, the seeds of its revival were sown in the 1829 Act of Emancipation, in which all restrictions on Roman Catholics were lifted, they could worship freely and take an active role in political and public life. The following year, the Oxford Movement began, which concentrated the minds of theologians and academics on the state of the Church of England as it was at that time. The Oxford Movement was led by Newman (later Cardinal Newman), Keble, Pusey and others. As a result of the Oxford Movement, Anglo-Catholicism developed within the Church of England, bringing back with it such customs as the wearing of vestments, the use of incense, confessions, the rosary, candles and a much more ritualistic form of worship into the services. This did not have a great effect upon Walsingham until the end of the 19th century.

In 1894 an Anglo-Catholic called Miss Charlotte Pearson Boyd decided to follow the old pilgrim route from London to Walsingham. This time stopping at one ruined priory or wayside chapel after another. When she reached the Slipper Chapel, at Houghton St. Giles, she found it in a very dilapidated state, being used as a cow shed (it had been used for a variety of activities since the Dissolution). Charlotte Pearson Boyd decided she would buy the Chapel from the Lee Warners, the overall lords of the manor, restore it and put in a order of nuns. By the time she had completed negotiations to buy the Chapel in 1896 for £400, she had become a Roman Catholic.

On Thursday 19th August 1897 the Guild of Our Lady of Ransom organised the first revived Pilgrimage to the newly built Roman Catholic Church of St. Mary's in King's Lynn, which contained a chapel dedicated to Our Lady of Walsingham, and on Friday 20th August to Walsingham and the Slipper Chapel. Charlotte Boyd restored the Slipper Chapel and gave it to Downside Abbey. She died in April 1906.

In 1921 a new Anglican Priest was appointed to Walsingham. His name was Father Alfred Hope Patten. He was determined to establish Walsingham as a place for Anglican Pilgrims. He set up a copy of the Statue of Our Lady in the Guild's Chapel in the Parish Church and in 1922 organised the first Anglican Pilgrimage. By 1931 Fr. Hope Patten had enough support to build the Anglican Shrine, which contains a replica of the Holy House to the exact dimensions we know from William of Worcester and Erasmus's accounts. Fr. Hope Patten finding the footings of an older building, was convinced that he was rebuilding the Shrine on the site of the original Chapel. However an extensive archaeological dig in 1961 within the grounds of the Priory, confirmed that the site for the Holy House, was on the north wall of the Priory Church.

As the flow of pilgrims increased, so Walsingham began to wake up as a Pilgrimage centre. Fr. Hope Patten enlarged the Anglican Shrine Church in 1938. In 1934 the Slipper Chapel was redesignated the 'National Shrine of Our Lady of Walsingham.' Since 1934 pilgrims have been coming back in their thousands to Walsingham every year. By the late 1970s there were so many pilgrims visiting the Slipper Chapel it was necessary to build a larger chapel next to it, and in 1982 the Chapel of Reconciliation was consecrated.

The village once again thrives on the pilgrim trade - hostelries, gift shops, tea shops and coach parks! The wheel of history has come full circle and I am sure that most of the pilgrims who come to Walsingham today, come for spiritual help and guidance, and are putting forward the same petitions which Erasmus expressed in 1514:

> The Health of my family, the increase of my estate,
> a long and happy life in this world, and eternal
> happiness in the next.

REFERENCES

1. The Pynson Ballad - Pepys Library, Magdalene College, Cambridge.
2. Walsingham Charter - Cotton MS. Nero E.VII. See Dugdale, Monasticon Anglicanum.
3. Desiderius Erasmus, Pilgrimage to St. Mary's Walsingham & St. Thomas Canterbury. Translated by John Gough Nichols (1849).
4. B. M. Nero E. VII Fos. 173-174; J. C. Dickinson, Shrine of Our Lady of Walsingham (1956) p.136.
5. Dickinson op. cit., p.17-19
6. Dickinson op. cit., p.28-33.
7. Bodleian Library, Oxford. MS Rawl. Poet 219 fo.
8. Itineraria. Willelmi de Worcester Ed. J. Nasmith (1778)
9. Letters and Papers... 11 (2) 1451; Dickinson op. cit., p.44.
10. Erasmus op. cit.; Dickinson op. cit., p.47.
11. Pat. 21 Edward III, pt i, m 28; Pat 22 Edward III pt i, m. 48; H. M. Gillett, Walsingham (1946) p.34-35
12. L. and P. No. 40; Dickinson op. cit., p.44.
13. Calendar of Patent Rolls (1361-4), 473-44; Dickinson op. cit., p.26-27.
14 The Paston Papers ed. Roger Virgoe p. 44.
15. L. and P. ii (2) No. 3655, 3670; Dickinson op. cit., p.45
16. Chronica (RS79) ii 76-7; Thomas of Walsingham, Historia Anglorum (RS 79). Dickinson op. cit., p.20
17. Anglica Historia 25; Dickinson op. cit., p.42
18. L and P. Hen VIII Ii 1786; Gillett op. cit., p.43
19. The Book of Margery Kempe. (1985) Trans. B. A. Windealt
20. Thomas Percy, Bishop of Dromore, Reliques of Ancient English Poetry, (1765). Rev. L. E. Whatmore, Highway to Walsingham (1973) p.8.
21. Whatmore op. cit., p.22
22. Whatmore op. cit., p.34
23. H. J. Hillen, History of The Borough of Lynn. Vol. 1. (1907) p.256
24. J. Adair, The Pilgrims Way (1978) p.115
25. Whatmore op. cit., p.60
26. Paston Letters ed. Jas Gairdner Vol. V. (1900) p.248
27. "The Old Bridge of Attleborough" by T. D. Atkinson. Norfolk Archaeology, Vol. XVIII (1945).
28. The Canterbury Tales. Geoffrey Chaucer - The Prologue
29. CPR 12578-66 p. 182. P.R.O. Whatmore op. cit.,
30. Visitation of The Diocese of Lincoln (1517-31) Vol. 1. ed. A. D. Hamilton Thompson, Lincoln Record Soc., From Atwater Mss fol. 47; Whatmore op. cit., p.2.
31. Dickinson op. cit.
32. W. Richards, History of Lynn Vol. 1 (1812). p.563
33. From M. S. Cotton Cleop. E.IV Fol 231-LXIII. Letters from Richard Southwell to Cromwell.
34. F. Blomefield, History of Norfolk Vol. IX (1808) p.280.
35. Hillen op. cit.

36. Edward M. Beloe, Red Mount Chapel 'Our Lady's Hill, Lynn, and the Chapels Thereon' (1889).
37. Rev. Edward Edwards, The Chapel of Our Lady on the Mount, or Red Mount; Hillen op. cit.
38. Richard le Strange, Monasteries of Norfolk. (1973)
39. Whatmore, op. cit., p.62-63
40. Valor Ecclesiasticus (Rec. Com) III 385-8.
41. Dickinson, op. cit.
42. Norfolk Archaeological Society "Opposition to the Suppression of the Norfolk Monasteries and Expression of Discontent - The Walsingham Conspiracy" by T. H. Swales, MA.
43. Le Strange, op. cit., p.124
44. Dickinson, op. cit., p.67
45. Le Strange op. cit.

PILGRIMAGE AND THE SICK IN MEDIEVAL EAST ANGLIA

by Dr. Carole Rawcliffe

> A certain well-known man of Norwich had himself phlebotomised on a particular occasion. But he neglected to take the necessary measures for post-operative care; and as a result found it impossible to sleep. I need not here expound on the virtues and blessings of sleep ... for rest conserves the health and nature not only of men, but also of beasts. This wretched individual passed almost seven years without a night's sleep. And, by and by, his muscles contracted; he grew pale and lean and shrivelled, and his mouth was all discoloured; and those who beheld him seemed able to count all the bones in his body. His sorrow and incapacity were compounded by poverty, in so far that he had previously been rich in friends as well as money, but was now destitute of both and forced to lie idle. For he could provide neither for himself nor his dependents. In the seventh year of his misfortune, when the relics of St. Bartholomew's Hospital Church were brought and placed in the oratory of St. Nicholas's Church in Yarmouth, this man approached them devoutly, and meekly prostrating himself asked and sought remedy. He found what he sought, and applied at the door, and the porter opened it, and behaved mercifully towards him. Grovelling on the ground, he increased his prayers and began to sleep. And after he had slept for a long time, he arose whole, and went back home, giving thanks to God who mortifies and revives, smites down and heals.[1]

So runs a 12th century account of one of the many miracles vouchsafed to the hopeful pilgrims who flocked in large numbers to venerate the fragment of the True Cross and other relics on display at St. Bartholomew's Hospital in London, and at the various places where they were exhibited for the benefit of those in search of physical or spiritual wellbeing. In this tale we find all the elements which make the subject of pilgrimage so fascinating to the medical historian: the deployment of relics as the focus of a healing cult; the evident risks and inadequacies of earthly medicine; despair in the face of a debilitating, but fairly unspecific disorder of the kind likely to be psychogenic, or self-limiting or at least liable to periods of remission; and, above all, a conviction that God alone, through the medium of his son or of his saints, could preserve or restore health.

It was this last which ensured the primacy of spiritual over earthly medicine throughout the medieval period, and which, as we shall see in the course of this essay, is entirely understandable in an age without antisepsis, antibiotics, blood transfusion, reliable anaesthesia, vitamin supplements, x-rays, microscopes or any of the other advances in medical science readily available in the West today. Men and women were urged to put their faith in treatment of a very different kind:

> As Christians we know that there are two kinds of medicine, one of earthly things, the other of heavenly things. They differ in both origin and efficacy. Through long experience, earthly doctors learn the powers of herbs and the like, which alter the condition of human bodies. But there has never been a doctor so experienced in this art that he has not found some illnesses difficult to cure and others completely incurable ... The author of heavenly medicine is Christ, who could heal the sick with a command and raise the dead from the grave.[2]

Theologians, from St. Augustine onwards, often described Christ as the divine physician, *Christus Medicus*, who heals the cancer and leprosy of sin in all sick souls, as well as attending to more immediate bodily infirmities.[3]

It is worth noting the frequency of this terminology in medieval religious writing. A hagiographical compilation entitled *The Life, Passion and Miracles of St. Edmund, King and Martyr* records, for instance, the case of a young woman with a swelling on her breast who elected, after conventional medical treatment had made her worse, to invoke the *Celestus Medicus*. He, in turn, referred her to his junior partner, "the glorious martyr," St. Edmund, at the Benedictine abbey in Bury.[4] On many occasions the saints themselves are described as *medici*: another source recounts a vision in which the two physicians, St. Edmund and St. Thomas Becket, reputedly appeared together to a sick man to deliver a stern warning about the dangers of excessive dependence on man-made pills and potions.[5] The story of Elias, a leprous monk from Reading, whose disease proved impervious to the healing waters at Bath but responded immediately to water containing infinitesimal drops of Becket's blood, is typical of the genre. "He set his hope in the warmth of the sulphur and not in the wonder-working martyr," admonished the chronicler, William of Canterbury, and was cured only when he ceased to look for an earthly remedy.[6]

The miraculous cure of a blind child after a pilgrimage to the relics of St. Louis. Note that the boy and his father wear the conventional dress of pilgrims, with badges in their hats. On the left hand side the pair undertake their journey; on the right the boy recovers his sight and is able to identify objects.

In *The Canterbury Tales*, Geoffrey Chaucer draws attention to the academic credentials of his physician-pilgrim, which derive entirely from classical medical authorities and the Arab and Hebrew scholars who wrote commentaries on them. He does not spend much time reading the Bible, but is learned in the texts of Galen, Avicenna and Hippocrates, and is thus essentially a theoretician, whose principal concern is the prevention of disease through the management of his patients' diet and lifestyle.[7] In some respects, the type of holistic therapy practised by medieval physicians seems remarkably enlightened to a late 20th century audience. With its emphasis on moderation and the need for careful balance, the traditional *regimen* had much to recommend it. But once a patient fell ill, treatment could be extremely unpleasant and unpredictable, as well as expensive.[8] Chaucer's physician has about him all the trappings of material success:

> In blood-red garments, slashed with bluish grey
> And lined with taffeta he rode his way:
> Yet he was rather close in his expenses
> And kept the gold he won in pestilences.
> Gold stimulates the heart, or so we're told.
> He therefore had a special love of gold.[9]

As satirists well knew, however, even the greatest and most influential of court physicians was powerless in the face of Death. And for this reason illustrations from the *Danse Macabre* [Dance of Death] frequently depicted an encounter between the two ill-matched protagonists, one draped in expensive fur, the other beckoning gleefully with a skeletal finger.[10]

If physic offered little hope of recovery, surgery, as we have already seen, constituted even more of a gamble. Many presumed miracles concerned the restoration to health of people who had been incompetently or excessively phlebotomised, among them being John de Kirkby, Bishop of Ely, who apparently went mad in 1290, after being bled too heavily by his barber. St. Etheldreda, whose shrine lay in the cathedral, took pity upon him and restored him to health, but his vicious lifestyle brought divine retribution in the end.[11] What price physical wellbeing if the soul remained infected?

Shrine keepers enjoyed reporting botched phlebotomies and failed attempts at medication, as they showed how little reliance could be placed in earthly medicine. The Church used healing cults as a means of establishing its power and authority, and thus secured without much opposition that place on the pedestal occupied today by bio-medicine and 'big science.' But saintly practitioners were not always infallible: just like their earthly counterparts they could misdiagnose symptoms or bungle operations, in which case it seemed worth soliciting a second opinion. The sick knight who dreamt that the Virgin Mary, St. Leonard and St. Edmund performed abdominal surgery on him in his sleep was relieved that St. Thomas Becket was on hand to spot the corrupt matter they had missed.[12] Displaying a robust pragmatism somewhat at odds with their apparent credulity, medieval pilgrims were quite prepared to 'shop around' in the saintly as well as the medical marketplace, visiting one centre after another until they experienced some improvement.

Indeed, the shrine keepers who recorded their experiences liked nothing better than to crow about a triumph over the competition. Imagine the delight at the comparatively modest shrine of St. Walstan at Bawburgh, just outside Norwich, when a Canterbury weaver who had repeatedly but unsuccessfully begged St. Thomas to cure his lameness was finally able to throw away his crutches on the way to Norfolk.[13] The monks of Bury can hardly have been any less jubilant when, in about 1095, one Wulmar, who had been struck down with paralysis on returning from a pilgrimage to Rome, and had actually received the *viaticum*, was restored to health after calling upon their very own St. Edmund.[14]

A significant number of reputed cures, rescues and resuscitations were effected at long distance, often after some kind of dream or vision, or while the pilgrim was still on the road. Some people, such as a certain woman who had lain for over a year "swollen and ulcerated as though afflicted with elephantiasis" at Brichtiu's Hospital in Norwich, were simply too sick to travel. At a convenient point between 1150 and 1173, just as his propagandist, Thomas of Monmouth, was busy promoting the cult of his relics at the cathedral priory, 'Little William,' the alleged victim of a Jewish conspiracy, appeared to her in a vision with the promise of healing and she became whole.[15] One of the miracles attributed to St. Edmund recounts how an old man from Northumberland, blind from his youth, travelled to Bury with friends and neighbours. Some distance from the town, but within sight of the tall bell-tower, they knelt to pray, at which point the man's sight was restored and he, rather than his servant, was able to lead the party towards the abbey.[16] Such tales, carefully recorded and no doubt embellished by the shrine-keepers, were a potent stimulus to pilgrimage. For the journey itself constituted a profession of faith (especially if one found travel painful or difficult), and was a crucial stage in the process of spiritual healing. Personal histories of fortitude in the face of suffering added, moreover, to that sense of pathos and drama which rendered the final outcome all the more impressive.[17]

Close physical proximity to a saint's earthly remains was, however, the ultimate goal of the medieval pilgrim. So much so that officiating clergy were obliged to issue harsh warnings against theft or desecration: it was by no means uncommon for visitors to break off fragments of a shrine - or even of a sacred relic - for medical use or crude material gain. There was, as Elias the monk discovered, an almost insatiable demand for holy water in which the remains of saints or other sanctified objects had been immersed, since it could be taken home for deployment in a myriad of healing rituals or for general protection against disease.[18] In this regard, as in so many others, shrine keepers were more likely to indulge the rich and powerful. Moved by a "fervour of pious devotion," the Lady Mabel de Bec was permitted to remove a small portion of the tomb of William of Norwich in the Cathedral so that it could be ground to powder as a sort of sacred cement and then mixed with water for internal or external use in medical emergencies.

> This she was careful to guard with the utmost diligence, since she thought it likely to produce often for herself and her children a fruitful outcome of her faith. And as she so confidently hoped, so it happened, for whenever she or her children experienced any inconvenient complaint, she resorted at once to the remedy in which she had confidence and which her faith had provided for her.[19]

With remarkable candour, Thomas of Monmouth describes how he slipped two of William's teeth into his own sleeve when the body was translated, contrasting his "pious theft" with the prior's churlish refusal to decorate the new sepulchre with a carpet. So far as Thomas was concerned the latter's early death allowed only one interpretation: he had grievously offended the boy martyr and thus deserved to be punished.[20] A less terrible, but more appropriate fate befell the irreligious Fleming who tried to bite off some of the lavish gold ornament on St. Edmund's shrine at Bury and could not withdraw his teeth from the casing. Saints might be vengeful as well as compassionate.[21]

The body parts, clothes and possessions of saints and other holy men and women were believed to emit an aura of sanctity which would, under the right circumstances, facilitate both physical and spiritual healing. Thus, a young woman with an ulcerated breast began to feel better after modelling an *ex voto* offering to William of Norwich out of warm wax (and thus applying a soothing poultice to the sores); but her eventual recovery was ascribed by Thomas of Monmouth to the fact that she had leaned against his tomb.[22] The decapitated head of the Anglo Saxon martyr, St. Edmund, miraculously attached to its body in an ornate shrine at the abbey church at Bury, was famed for a plethora of such miracles, often after the sick had drunk holy water from the saint's cup.[23]

A fifteenth-century depiction of the elaborately decorated shrine of St. Edmund at Bury St. Edmunds. The kneeling figure is King Henry VI on pilgrimage.

But what could one do when the body had already been taken up on high? During the later Middle Ages, as devotion to Christ and his mother was fostered by the Church and avidly embraced by the laity, shrines displaying sacred artefacts and miracle-working images assumed cult status. As a greater sensitivity with regard to the consumption of water or wine laced with real human detritus became apparent, men and women sought consolation in graphic depictions of Christ's suffering.[24] Not surprisingly, fragments of the True Cross, such as those sent from St. Bartholomew's Hospital to Yarmouth, or acquired (under extremely dubious circumstances from the medieval equivalent of a travelling salesman) by the Cluniacs at Bromholm on the Norfolk coast, were deemed to emit an especially potent brand of "holy radioactivity." At Bromholm, the chronicler, Roger of Wendover, recounts a catalogue of miracles similar to those described in the New Testament: "The dead came alive, the crippled recovered their mobility, the flesh of lepers was cleansed, the possessed were freed of their demons, and every single individual who approached the said wood [of the Cross] with faith withdrew again whole and well."[25]

As the cult of the Virgin Mary swept Europe, pilgrimage centres dedicated to her began to mushroom. Since she had joined her son in heaven, her physical remains were confined to tears and milk, such as the suspiciously chalky-looking matter which Erasmus found on display at Walsingham.[26] But as mediatrix on behalf of sinful humanity, her image alone could become a focus of popular devotion and healing. One such stood in the Lady Chapel built and adorned in the mid 15th century by John Clopton at Long Melford in Suffolk, which was approached by a wide ambulatory allowing plenty of room for pilgrims. In 1529 the statue of the Virgin there was festooned with votive offerings, including rings, jewels and silver spoons.[27] The Benedictine monks of Norwich set up three such Marian shrines in the Cathedral during the 14th century, hoping to counteract the declining appeal (and material value) of St. William. Neither they, nor any of the other relics purchased at this time, however, attracted the sick in significant numbers: although it might be nurtured from above, the response had to come freely from below.[28] Thomas More recounts how the daughter of Sir Roger Wentworth was apparently released from daemonic possession before a large crowd at the more famous shrine of the Blessed Virgin in Ipswich:

> ... being brought and laid before the image of our Blessed Lady, [she] was there in the sight of many worshipful people so grievously tormented and in face, eyes, look and countenance so grievously changed, with her mouth drawn aside and her eyes fallen out upon her cheeks, that it was a terrible sight to behold. And after many astonishing things inflicted by the devil upon certain individuals, through God's sufferance, both the said individuals and the girl herself were restored perfectly and suddenly to their senses before all the company.[29]

In the intense, claustrophobic atmosphere of a shrine, heady with the smell of incense and the shimmer of candles, outbreaks of mass hysteria can hardly have been uncommon.

It was in the hope of undergoing just such a healing experience that thousands of men, women and children throughout medieval Europe embarked each year upon pilgrimages. Many would be clutching, or would purchase on arrival, wax images of diseased or painful body parts as *ex voto* offerings, pledged to the saint either in the hope of a cure or because one had already taken place. In 1475-76, the chandlers of York (many of whom doubled up as barber-surgeons) got into trouble for aggressive marketing of 'ymages' along the road to the minster.[30] The Canterbury weaver, whose successful cure on the way to Bawburgh is described above, deemed it expedient to fulfil his vow regarding the pledge of an *ex voto*:

> A leg of wax he had made there
> According to the counsel of his friend.
> In his arm he carried it
> To Bawburgh, and laid it down
> Before Saint Walstan, and devoutly prayed.
> Many folk saw him leave
> Hale and hearty and sure of foot.[31]

Wealthier pilgrims might wish to present a silver, gold or bejewelled *ex voto* instead. The shrine of the Blessed Virgin at Walsingham dripped jewels and shone with the glow of candlelight on plate, so lavish was the patronage bestowed upon it. When John Paston fell ill in London in 1443, his mother-in-law despatched what was evidently a second (or even third) "ymmage of wax" of his exact weight to Walsingham, while his wife arranged to make a pilgrimage there on his behalf.[32] On arriving at the same shrine a decade later to pray for an heir, Margaret of Anjou, Queen to Henry VI, presented "a tablet of gold garnished at the borders ... with ten tronches of pearl, five sapphires and five spinel rubies of rose-red, with an angel in the middle having at the head a cameo ... and holding between its hands a cross garnished with a ruby and nine oriental pearls."[33] It was worth £29, hardly a negligible sum, but small beer compared with the gem-encrusted image of the Annunciation valued at £266 given to the chapel at Walsingham by Henry, Earl of Lancaster, or the collection of plate to the same value made over by his son, the first Duke.[34] The latter was, incidentally, author of a celebrated tract on spiritual healing, entitled *The Book of Sacred Medicines*, which itemised the best means of combatting the infection of sin.[35]

By one of those striking ironies, of which the history of Christianity furnishes so many examples, the shrine of St. Walstan, a king turned ploughman who had given almost everything he possessed to the poor, went the same way. So numerous were the offerings made at Bawburgh church in the 13th century that by 1309 there were sufficient resources to rebuild and lavishly adorn the chancel, providing space for six chantry priests to celebrate mass for pilgrims as well as patrons.[36] Whether crafted out of wax or solid gold, a notable proportion of these gifts were a tangible manifestation of real human pain. It is sobering to reflect that papal commissioners visiting the tomb of Thomas Cantelupe at Hereford Cathedral, during the canonization process of 1307, found over 2,000 models of whole bodies or limbs, 108 discarded walking sticks and crutches, ninety-five children's shifts and "an uncountable quantity of eyes, breasts, teeth and ears."[37]

Each of the 19 or so most celebrated healing shrines of medieval Norfolk would have attracted similar donations.[38] We should remember that for a significant number of pilgrims the journey was, if not a matter of life and death, a desperate attempt to regain lost health. Few pilgrimages were quite as agreeable or diverting as the one described so vividly by Geoffrey Chaucer. Although there can be no doubt that many people regarded a pilgrimage as a holiday, and thus felt all the better for a change of scenery, comparatively few pilgrims were as fit and carefree as this party of travellers. A significant proportion, by contrast, were severely disabled and in great pain. Several such cases are itemised among the miracles of William of Norwich (c.1170). Even allowing for the customary embellishments, they reveal a faith born of desperation. One account concerns a crippled woman who dragged herself on trestles a few inches at a time all the way from Langham near Holt to the martyr's tomb in the Cathedral. She had previously been transported to shrines by her vicar slung over the back of his horse, but on this occasion she wanted to give proof of her devotion by proceeding unassisted.[39] Another tells the story of a cripple who travelled on foot over 180 miles from York:

> ... very weak throughout his body, [he] guided his steps and supported his frame on two sticks such as are commonly called crutches. With the view of coming to the holy martyr to receive healing, he set out from York as best he could and, journeying slowly, spent many days over his long pilgrimage, supported on the way by faith and drawn on by hope.[40]

Where did all these people stay? One of the earliest and most pressing reasons to found a hospital was for the accommodation of pious wayfarers. In 6th century France conciliar decrees reminded senior clergy of their responsibilities in this regard, and hospices rapidly appeared along the major pilgrimage routes to Rome and Compostela. In England at least 136

A pilgrim makes an ex voto offering at the shrine of St. William of York. He has an injured leg and presents a wax model of it in the hope of being cured. On the left hang models of other body parts.

hospitals were specifically endowed for "the wayfaring poor of Christ," priority usually being accorded to pilgrims.[41] In Norfolk and Suffolk a network of such houses included the hospital of St. James at Horning (near the shrine of St. Theobald at Hautbois), a hostel outside the gates of the nearby abbey of St. Benet Hulme, another at the college of St. John the Baptist at Rushford, the hospital of St. Mary and St. Julian by the bridge at Thetford, and a Franciscan refuge at Walsingham. The Bury St. Edmunds chronicler, Jocelin of Brakelond, observed that St. Saviour's, the largest of the town's seven hospitals, was founded by Abbot Samson in about 1184, "that it might provide food for the poor and accommodation for travellers."[42]

All but the smallest pilgrim hospitals were served by a resident or nearby priest, who could offer penitents the benefits of confession and the mass, both of which were deemed to possess physical as well as spiritual healing properties.

Charity, personified as a woman, receives sick, tired and hungry pilgrims into her own home. Giving hospitality to strangers was one of the Seven Temporal Works, deemed to bestow spiritual health on the donor.

Private individuals, and especially women, were urged to take pilgrims into their own homes, receiving them as Christ's representatives on earth. In the 15th century English poem, *The Pilgrim*, which offers an allegory for life itself, the author recounts how:

> One there came and welcomed me,
> And her name was Charity,
> All pilgrims, in a cheerful way,
> She blessed and bade them freely stay.
> With cheer benign and glad usage
> She brought them to their herbergage.[43]

Such was the exemplar held up to all good Christians. In practice, however, the social, demographic and economic upheavals of the 14th century provoked a less than charitable reaction towards the vagrant poor and pilgrimage came to be seen as a soft option for the workshy. Many small hostels either closed or converted into wayside chapels, while the larger hospitals became increasingly reluctant to accommodate impoverished wayfarers of any kind.

The hospital of St. Thomas at Beck, near Walsingham, had, for instance, been founded during the reign of Henry III for the relief of thirteen pilgrims, but ceased to perform this function after the Black Death.[44] Well before then, inns had sprung up at all the major shrines, offering comparatively cheap accommodation. The destruction by fire of four inns at Walsingham, in 1431, was blamed upon pilgrims who resented the excessive prices.[45] Yet still they came, and there is nothing to suggest that numbers (and certainly not numbers of sick pilgrims) declined in any significant respect before the Reformation. At Thetford, where the Cluniac priory had housed a notable collection of healing relics (including a piece of wood said to come from the manger in Bethlehem), the burgesses complained in 1538 to Thomas Cromwell that the town had "always been greatly maintained, relieved and preserved by the resort and trade of pilgrims," but the Dissolution had brought them into "extreme beggary."[46]

In the last resort, sick people desperately wanted miracles, as Sir Thomas More, a by no means uncritical observer of early 16th century society, observed:

> Some priest, to attract pilgrims to his parish, may recruit a false fellow, pretending to be blind, to come and invoke the help of a saint in his church, and suddenly claim to have recovered his sight. Then he will have all the bells rung to announce a miracle. And the fond folk from the countryside are soon made fools. And the women flock hither with their candles. And the parson buys three or four pairs of old crutches from a lame beggar, and spends twelve pence on models of wax ... and his offerings are soon worth twice what he gets in tithes![47]

Like countless other hagiographers and shrine-keepers, Thomas of Monmouth records the arrival of anguished parents with their paralysed children on litters and stretchers and even in wheelbarrows. He lists all the cases of heart disease, dropsy, blindness, deafness, toothache, constipation, cancer, fever, daemonic possession, convulsions, epilepsy, sore eyes, deformity, ulcers, and wasting sickness which were miraculously cured through William's intervention. The exact nature of these "cures", and, of course, of the illnesses themselves, is open to debate; but few of us, however robustly sceptical of ecclesiastical propaganda, would deny that we are dealing here with powerful evidence about the strategies deployed by the sick of medieval Europe, and about their approach to illness and health.[48]

It is stating the obvious to stress that information about the workings and malfunction of the human body, which we take for granted, was simply not available to medieval men and women; but without it the miraculous suddenly seems far more plausible. For example, as late as 1797 *The Encyclopaedia Britannica* noted: "The signs of death are in many cases very uncertain ... between life and death the shade is so very undistinguishable that even all the powers of art can scarcely determine where the one ends and the other begins."[49] It then proceeded to warn against the dangers of premature burial in apparent cases of death by accident or drowning. Notwithstanding the availability of various tracts listing the tell-tale indications of approaching death, the problem was even greater in the Middle Ages, when superficial appearances were all that people had to rely on. William of Canterbury, one of the keepers at St. Thomas Becket's shrine, noted laconically that in England miraculous revivals from the dead were common after three days, but comparatively rare after a week.[50] This is hardly surprising given the speed with which burials then took place: but it does explain why so many relatively minor saints were held, like Christ, to possess the power to raise the dead. One such was St. Walstan of Bawburgh, who breathed life into a local thatcher. The latter had lain for two days, face upwards in a pond, apparently drowned, and had been placed in front of the Saint's tomb before burial.[51] It was there that he regained consciousness, to the consternation of his neighbours.

Thomas Gatele, an early 15th century sub-prior of Walsingham, claimed as a boy to have fallen down one of the two sacred wells at the shrine of the Blessed Virgin there, and to have been brought back from the dead through her miraculous intervention. To have swallowed so much holy water must have guaranteed him a long and healthy life.[52] Accident victims, apparently stillborn children and men and women who had collapsed without warning might be transported to the nearest shrine, where recovery would inevitably be seen as miraculous. Since it was, moreover, a common practice to invoke the name of a saint on such occasions, and to sprinkle the body with holy water, of the sort Lady Mabel de Bec kept about her person, resuscitations did not even have to occur at a shrine for the keepers to claim divine intervention.

Men, women and children who were fortunate enough to recover quickly from concussion following falls, industrial injuries and traffic accidents (medieval carts, with their iron-shod wheels, were fearsome vehicles) also seemed touched by God: an understandable reaction in an age when the outcome of medical or surgical intervention under such circumstances was rarely successful. One remarkable anecdote concerns the courtier, Sir James Berners, who was travelling to Walsingham on a pilgrimage with Richard II, in 1383, when the royal party encountered a thunderstorm at Ely and he was struck by lightening. Fortunately for him, the tomb of St. Etheldreda lay near at hand. Richard immediately ordered all the clergy to process to "the shrine of the great virgin," where his friend, "blind and half-crazed" by a vision of the Last Judgement, regained all his faculties.[53]

Recovery from temporary concussion must have appeared strikingly dramatic. But, the eloquence of the hagiographers notwithstanding, few reputed miracles seemed quite so clear-cut or immediate. Indeed, two important factors influenced popular perceptions of exactly what constituted a "cure".

Firstly, expectations were infinitely lower than they are today. We know from the numerous medical negligence cases to survive from the later Middle Ages that the boundary between sickness and health was ill-defined and fluid: the restoration of limited mobility or lessening of pain was often all a patient hoped for. One case, heard in the petty pleas at Ipswich, in 1415, involved a failed attempt to treat blindness, the criterion for success established at the outset being that the plaintiff would be able to distinguish one colour from another.[54] It is, of course, quite possible to do this while still remaining visually impaired. Success was entirely subjective, and might prove short-lived. Chronic toothache and constipation, ubiquitous features of medieval life, clearly fell into this category, as did malaria and other diseases characterised by intermittent bouts of fever. Even when the process of canonization was involved, no sustained attempt was made to monitor the pilgrim's progress after he or she had returned home.

Secondly, we should remember the derivation of the word 'patient'. Living as they did in a world of suffering, disease and death, medieval men and women were accustomed to low level pain, and rarely expected instant results. They were prepared to trudge from one shrine to the next, in the hope that one day their faith would be rewarded and they would be deemed worthy of a cure. On arrival they settled down to wait, perhaps for weeks on end. Not surprisingly, those suffering from self-limiting complaints often felt better, as, no doubt, did many victims of psychosomatic disorders. The less fortunate were advised to accept God's will with humility. One of the many popular cautionary tales used by medieval preachers to enliven their sermons tells of a group of lame and deformed pilgrims who congregated for some days at a shrine, confident that at least one of them would be healed. Denied any miracle, they left noisily during the service, disrupting the divine office, and were stopped by the priest. Having ordered them to throw away their crutches, he announced that the most disabled member of the party would be burnt so that his ashes could be used to cure the rest. All hastily left the church unaided. "How wretched are those", ran the moral, "who fear and flee earthly fire, but have no dread of divine wrath".[55] Pilgrims knew better than to offend either God or his saints through displays of petulance.

Because the medical terminology deployed in the Middle Ages was so very different from our own, most latter-day attempts at diagnosis must at best remain impressionistic. Shrine keepers and hagiographers derived their understanding of human physiology from classical medical theory, with the result that, in the relatively few cases where a detailed account of physical symptoms is provided, illnesses tend to be described in terms of humoral imbalances or blockages, which the saint miraculously removed.[56] By and large, however, chroniclers employ an unspecific and limited vocabulary, without much in the way of elaboration: pilgrims are blind, or crooked, feverish, dropsical or afflicted with sores. The language is biblical: we are told little in the way of case histories.

One is, however, struck by the number of pathological conditions likely to disappear or enter periods of remission during the pilgrimage season in spring and summer. Far more common than it is today in the West, and ubiquitous in the records made by shrine-keepers, blindness was often a result of poor diet, parasitic infections and a dirty, smoke-filled domestic environment. Xerophthalmia, or temporary loss of vision, results from a lack of vitamin A in a cereal based diet of the kind generally consumed by the English peasantry during periods of high population density.[57] Among the miracles attributed to St. Edmund was the cure of a three-year-old girl who had been blind for five weeks, and of a young man whose sudden *malus in oculo* was regarded as a punishment for blasphemy, but probably had more to do with diet, if not hysteria. In the latter case, we are told that the charms and mutterings of old women proved powerless to help him, which serves as a reminder that most people's first recourse was to a wise woman or herbalist.[58]

Scurvy, another affliction endured by malnourished men and women, would clear up when Vitamin C became available, as would boils, running sores and many of the debilitating conditions loosely described by the shrine keepers under the general heading of 'ulcers'. The pains of osteo-arthritis became more bearable in warmer weather. Respiratory diseases and other infections likely to result from cold, damp winters spent without adequate clothing, heating or housing, might also show quite dramatic signs of improvement.[59] Contaminated or adulterated food caused intestinal problems at all levels of society, and especially among the poor. It has been argued that some of the more spectacular cases of violent daementia, where the sufferer was brought bound and chained to church, were, in fact, the result of ergotism, which is caused by poisoned rye. To contemporaries such terrifying behaviour offered indisputable evidence of demonic possession, which only God or his saints could bring to an end.[60] Several other conditions were class specific: an analysis of English shrines and their clientele undertaken by R. C. Finucane, in his important study of *Miracles and Pilgrims*, shows that, generally speaking, rich pilgrims were less likely to display symptoms of diseases associated with hard manual labour, dietary deficiencies and difficult living conditions, and that poor women, not surprisingly, were the most vulnerable of all.[61] They were also the group most likely to resort to the cult of saints at an early stage in the hierarchy of resort, while elite males would almost certainly turn first to earthly medication or surgery.

The threat to health of repeated pregnancies and the very real possibility of death in childbirth loomed large over all medieval women, whether queens or paupers, although malnutrition, deformity (perhaps as a result of childhood rickets) and squalid surroundings, shared with domestic animals, inevitably worsened the plight of the female poor.[62] An examination of skeletal material from one of the most deprived areas of medieval York, for example, reveals that adult women were lucky to reach their late thirties, dying, on average, some four or five years earlier than men. In 15th century Florence the chances of survival past 30 were slimmer for both sexes.[63] Children were even more vulnerable. Infant mortality, clearly affected by maternal health, was running at about 60% in the poorer parts of late Anglo-Saxon Norwich, and around 50% in similar communities in medieval York.[64] Sexually transmitted diseases bred of dirt, overcrowding and poverty clearly took their toll as well.[65]

As St. Augustine reminded his readers, the discomforts of pregnancy, suffering in childbirth, miscarriage, the loss of infants and maternal mortality were a bitter legacy, bequeathed by Eve to each of her daughters. But redemption was at hand, through the agency of Christ and his mother the Virgin, to whom women turned, with optimism as well as fear, at this dangerous time. They appealed to other saints as well, both male and female, for assistance during pregnancy and childbirth. One of the best-known accounts of a difficult medieval delivery involving a long labour and an awkward presentation is to be found among the recorded miracles of St. Thomas Becket, because it was to him that the midwives appealed. Needless to say, they received none of the credit for saving both mother and child, whose survival was attributed to divine intervention.[66]

During the 16th century English reforming bishops, who were responsible for the licensing of midwives, tried hard to prevent them from encouraging women in labour to invoke the protection of saints or relics, such as holy girdles reputedly worn by the Virgin or St. Mary Magdalen and occasionally hired out by shrine-keepers to royal or aristocratic women.[67] In his will of 1530, the Suffolk knight, Sir William Clopton, left a gold cross to his male heirs on condition that they agreed to lend it to "honest women being with child at the time of their labour".[68] The less well-connected had to make do with pilgrim badges or holy water from shrines, such as those at Ipswich or Walsingham, which attracted pregnant and infertile women alike. Many would have worn cheap metal badges depicting the Virgin and Child, or the Annunciation, or the Holy House of Walsingham (a wooden replica of the one in Nazareth where medieval men and women believed the Incarnation had begun) throughout pregnancy and during labour. As an elderly woman, Margery Kempe, herself the mother of fourteen children, travelled further afield to Cologne in 1433 to see "Our Lady's smock", which was believed to assist women in childbirth. She may well have returned with a badge similar to one fashioned into an ornate pendant unearthed in Pottergate, Norwich, depicting the *sancta roba*, hanging beside the Virgin and Child.[69]

A fifteenth-century pewter badge of Christ and the Virgin from Walsingham.

The lollards attacked such beliefs as profoundly superstitious, and their views were vigorously espoused by Protestant reformers in the 16th century. In 1538, the evangelical Bishop of Salisbury, Nicholas Shaxton, who became master of the Great Hospital, Norwich, warned the midwives in his diocese to cease urging women "in travail to make any foolish vow to go on pilgrimage to this image or that image", but he faced an uphill struggle.[70] Obstetrics, as the French surgeon, Guy de Chauliac, scornfully noted, was a "field haunted by women", when the arrival of the male practitioner almost invariably spelt death.[71] Although the fifteen days' labour reputedly endured in 1144 by Botilda, wife of the cook employed by the Norwich Benedictines, was far from typical, her recourse to such measures as water in which sacred relics had been dipped, and a piece of fern removed from the bier of William, the boy martyr, seems fairly representative.[72]

In this respect, as in so many others, pilgrimage was comfortably absorbed into an ancient, pre-Christian tradition of folk healing through the use of amulets, incantations and sacred objects, which the medieval Church attempted to harness for its own purposes of social control. This it did remarkably well - at least by the standards of its own propaganda, which was disseminated with great professionalism and bravura. It held a strong hand of cards. In a pre-Cartesian world, when body and soul appeared inseparably joined, the one constantly held to determine the state of the other, what we might describe as psychosomatic disorders clearly responded especially well to the highly ritualised and cathartic experience of pilgrimage. This symbiotic relationship was reinforced by the powerful argument that sin could, and frequently did, cause disease. One of the most celebrated decrees of the Fourth Lateran council of 1215 insisted upon confession *before* medical treatment for this very reason, observing that "just as the cause ceases so does the effect". Another of its rulings advised the confessor to be

> ... discerning and prudent, so that *like a skilled physician* he may pour wine and oil over the wounds of the injured one. Let him carefully inquire about the circumstances of both the sinner and the sin, so that he may prudently discern what sort of advice he ought to give and *what remedy to apply, using various means to heal the sick person.*[73]

For all devout Christians (and these are the ones we know about), confession and absolution were a essential precursor to pilgrimage, which required a clean soul and a contrite heart. And confession, as many physicians observed, might prompt an immediate improvement in bodily health.[74] It is important to remember that a pilgrimage offered far more than physical wellbeing: along with the prospect of *spiritual fitness,* came the promise of release from the pains of purgatory or the eternal fires of hell. A dissolute knight who fell sick was urged to *confess his sins and make a pilgrimage* to St. Edmund's tomb, where his lacerated, festering soul as well his sick body would be cured. Another wealthy knight, sunk in vice (clearly there is some social justice at work here), entreated the saint to perform the ultimate miracle by restoring him to spiritual health, just as he helped others to regain physical strength.[75] It was to "expiate their offences" that hundreds of pilgrims poured "almost daily" into the shrine of the Virgin Mary outside Merevale Abbey, in Warwickshire, during the plague of 1361, dying there in considerable numbers because, ironically, the intense and desperate crush of people provided ideal conditions for the spread of infection.[76] Pilgrimage was widely recommended as a prophylactic against the plague (itself seen as divine punishment for sin) and as a means of warding off that other horseman of the apocalypse, famine: whatever social, economic and medical problems it may have exacerbated, it at least gave ordinary men and women some sense of purpose and control when the odds were so heavily stacked against them.

Because of Chaucer's genius as a storyteller it is easy to forget that *The Canterbury Tales* is more than just a collection of diverting anecdotes told by men and women with time on their hands as they travelled to the shrine of St. Thomas. It is no less than a metaphor for life itself as a great pilgrimage "called the celestial to Jerusalem". According to some commentators, it should end on a sombre note, with a prose sermon from the Parson on the subject of confession and sin. In the church of Holy Trinity, Long Melford, above the image of the Virgin and her lavish *ex voto* offerings, were painted verses by the Bury St. Edmunds monk, John Lydgate. These served to remind the 15th century reader (as if it were necessary) of the transitory, ephemeral nature of human life. Time in this vale of tears was short.

> Tarry no longer towards thy heritage
> Haste on thy way and be of right good cheer
> Go each day onwards on thy pilgrimage
> Think how short time thou hast abided here.[77]

If the sick pilgrim returned home as ulcerated, feverish or lame as he or she had started out, there was, at least, some prospect of health in the life to come.

REFERENCES

1. N. Moore, ed., The Book of the Foundation of St Bartholomew's Hospital, Early English Text Society, Vol. clxiii, (1923) p.27.
2. A hymn written in the eleventh century to St Pantaleon: K. Park, "Medicine and Society in Medieval Europe", in A. Wear, ed., Medicine in Society, Cambridge (1992) p.64. See also, S. R. Ell, The Two Medicines, Janus, Vol. lxviii (1981) pp.15-23.
3. R. Arbesmann, "The Concept of Christus Medicus in St Augustine", Traditio, Vol. x (1954) pp.1 -20.
4. T. Arnold, ed., Memorials of St Edmund's Abbey, 3 vols, Rolls Series, London (1890-96) vol. i, p.374.
5. R. C. Finucane, Miracles and Pilgrims, New York (1995) p.67.
6. J. C. Robertson, ed., Materials for the History of Thomas Becket, 7 vols, Rolls Series, London (1875-88) vol. ii, p.242. Elias's abbot, we are told for good measure, did not honour Becket as he should, and had a stubborn faith in medical practice.
7. F. N. Robinson, ed., The Works of Geoffrey Chaucer, Oxford (1970) p.21.
8. For an account of the work of the medieval physician, see C. Rawcliffe, Medicine and Society in Later Medieval England, Stroud (1995) pp. 105-24.
9. Modern translation by Neville Coghill, The Canterbury Tales, London (1992) p.23.
10. Rawcliffe, Medicine and Society, plate 15 and pp.116-17.
11. Bartholomew Cotton, Historia Anglicana, ed. H. R. Luard, Rolls Series, London (1859) p.174.
12. Finucane, Miracles and Pilgrims, p.68.
13. M. R. James, "Lives of St Walstan", Norfolk Archaeology, Vol. xix (1917) pp.262-63. See also C. Twinch, In Search of St Walstan, Norwich (1995) for a general discussion of the history of this cult.
14. Arnold, Memorials of St Edmund's Abbey, vol. i, pp. 160-62.
15. Thomas of Monmouth, The Life and Miracles of St William of Norwich, eds A. Jessopp and M. R. James, Cambridge (1896) p.148. For background, see G. I. Langmuir, "Thomas of Monmouth: Detector of Ritual Murder", Speculum, Vol. lvi (1984) pp.820-56.
16. Arnold, Memorials of St Edmund's Abbey, vol. i, pp.371 -72.
17. B. Ward, Miracles and the Medieval Mind, Aldershot (1987) p.35.
18. J. Sumption, Pilgrimage: An Image of Medieval Religion, London (1975) pp.82-83.
19. Thomas of Monmouth, Life and Miracles of St William, pp.135-36.
20. Ibid., pp.122-23, 127, 165-66.
21. Arnold, Memorials of St Edmund's Abbey, vol. i, pp.373-74.
22. Thomas of Monmouth, Life and Miracles of St William, pp.253-54.
23. As, for example, the girl with the swelling on her breast, who drank three times from his cup in the name of the Trinity: Arnold, Memorials of St Edmund's Abbey, vol. i, p.374, and also p.191.
24. Sumption, Pilgrimage, pp.82-83.
25. F. Wormald, "The Rood of Bromholm", Journal of the Warburg Institute, Vol. i (1937-38) pp.31-45; Roger of Wendover, Flores Historiarum, ed. H. G. Hewlett, 3 vols, Rolls Series, London (1886-98) vol. ii, pp.274-76.

26. Desiderius Erasmus, Colloquies, ed. C. R. Thompson, Collected Works of Erasmus XL, University of Toronto Press (1997) pp.632-33.
27. G. McMurray Gibson, The Theater of Devotion: East Anglian Drama and Society in the Late Middle Ages, Chicago (1989) pp.84-86.
28. J. R. Shinners, "The Veneration of Saints at Norwich Cathedral in the Fourteenth Century", Norfolk Archaeology, Vol. xl (1987) p.138.
29. Thomas More, A Dialogue Concerning Heresies, ed. T. M. C. Lawler, Complete Works of Thomas More VI, Yale University Press (1981) p.93.
30. Rawcliffe, Medicine and Society, pp.21-24.
31. James, "Lives of St Walstan", p.262-63.
32. N. Davis, ed., Paston Letters and Papers of the Fifteenth Century, 2 vols, Oxford (1971-76) vol. i, p.218.
33. A. R. Myers, "The Jewels of Queen Margaret of Anjou", Bulletin of the John Rylands Library, Vol. xlii (1959-60) pp.115, 124.
34. J. C. Dickinson, The Shrine of Our Lady at Walsingham, Cambridge (1956) pp.38-39.
35. E. J. Arnould, ed., Le Livre de Seyntz Medicines, Oxford (1940).
36. Twinch, St Walstan, pp.62-64.
37. Finucane, Miracles and Pilgrims, p.98.
38. These shrines are listed in R. Hart, "The Shrines and Pilgrimages of Norfolk", Norfolk Archaeology, Vol. vi (1864) pp.277-94.
39. Thomas of Monmouth, Life and Miracles of St William, pp.242-44.
40. Ibid., p.271.
41. C. Rawcliffe, The Hospitals of Medieval Norwich, Studies in East Anglian History, Vol. ii (1995) p.l35.
42. Ibid., p.142.
43. British Library Department of Manuscripts, Cottonian Ms Tiberius A VII, fo. 90. Reproduced in R. M. Clay, The Mediaeval Hospitals of England London, reprint 1966, plate 1.
44. Rawcliffe, Hospitals of Medieval Norwich, p.136; H. A. Doubleday, ed., The Victoria History of the County of Norfolk II London (1906) pp.438-39.
45. Dickinson, Our Lady of Walsingham, p.34.
46. D. Dymond, ed., The Register of Thetford Priory I Norfolk Record Society, Vol lix (1994) p.63.
47. Thomas More, A Dialogue Concerning Heresies, p.85.
48. For a wider discussion of this theme, see N. Siraisi, Medieval and Renaissance Medicine: An Introduction to Knowledge and Practice, Chicago (1990) pp.17-47.
49. Encyclopaedia Britannica, London (1797) pp.649-95.
50. Finucane, Miracles and Pilgrims, p.74.
51. James, Lives of Saint Walstan, p.261.
52. Dickinson, Our Lady of Walsingham, p.12.
53. L. C. Hetor and B. F. Harvey, eds, The Westminster Chronicle 1381-1394, Oxford (1982) p.43
54. Suffolk Record Office, Ipswich, C5/9 Petty Pleas, 2-3 Henry V.
55. T. F. Crane, ed., The Exempla of Jacques de Vitry Kraus reprint (1967) of Folk Lore Society, Vol. xxvi (1890) exemplum no. ccliv.

56. As, for example, Arnold, Memorials of St Edmund's Abbey, vol. i, pp.191, 374. For a useful discussion of medieval medical terminology, see P. Stell, Medical Practice in Medieval York, University of York, Borthwick Paper, No. xc (1996) pp.17-23.
57. Finucane, Miracles and Pilgrims, pp.106-7.
58. Arnold, Memorials of St Edmund's Abbey, vol i, pp.77-78, 83-84, 91-92, 109-10, 160, 181-82.
59. Stell, Medical Practice in Medieval York, p.21.
60. Finucane, Miracles and Pilgrims, pp.107-8. See also Thomas of Monmouth, Life and Miracles of St William, pp.203-5.
61. Finucane, Miracles and Pilgrims, pp.130-51.
62. H. Leyser, Medieval Women: A Social History of Women in England 450-1500, London (1995) pp.122-33.
63. J. D. Dawes and J. R. Magilton, The Cemetery of St Helen on the Walls, Aldwark, York Archaeological Trust (1980) p.63; Rawcliffe, Medicine and Society, p.4.
64. B. Ayers, ed., "Excavations within the North-East Bailey of Norwich Castle", East Anglian Archaeology, Vol. xxviii (1985) pp.49-58.
65. D. Jacquart and C. Thomasset, Sexuality and Medicine in the Middle Ages, Oxford (1988) pp.168-88.
66. Leyser, Medieval Women, pp.127-28.
67. Rawcliffe, Medicine and Society, pp.96, 180.
68. McMurray Gibson, Theater of Devotion, pp.61 -62.
69. S. Margerson, "Norwich Households: The Medieval and Post-Medieval Finds from Norwich Survey Excavations 1971-1978", East Anglian Archaeology, Vol. lviii (1993) p.8.
70. W. H. Frere and W. M. Kennedy, Visitation Articles and Injunctions 3 vols, London, (1910) vol. ii, p.58. He also warned parish priests not to encourage such "foolish devotion" as pilgrimages p.57. See also D. Cressy, Birth, Marriage and Death: Ritual, Religion and the Life Cycle in Tudor and Stuart England, Oxford (1997), pp.22-23, 64.
71. M. S. Ogden, ed., "The Cyrurgie of Guy de Chauliac", Early English Text Society, Vol. cclxv (1971) p.530.
72. Thomas of Monmouth, Life and Miracles of St William, pp.78-79.
73. N. Tanner, ed., Decrees of the Ecumenical Councils, 2 vols, Georgetown University Press (1990) vol. i, pp.245-46.
74. R. Palmer, "The Church, Leprosy and Plague in Medieval and Early Modern Europe", Studies in Church History XIX, Oxford (1982) p.86.
75. Arnold, Memorials of St Edmund's Abbey, pp.187-88, 204-7.
76. R. Horrox, ed., The Black Death, Manchester (1994) pp.148-49.
77. McMurray Gibson, Theater of Devotion, p.89.

THE FOUNDATION AND LATER HISTORY OF THE MEDIEVAL SHRINE

by Professor Christopher Harper-Bill

The Date of the Foundation

At the very end of the 15th century, when Walsingham was certainly the most renowned and popular pilgrimage centre in England, the printer Richard Pynson published a ballad which presented a narrative of the foundation and extolled the merits and efficacy of Our Lady of Walsingham.[1] In the first verse it is stated that the chapel was established in 1061, in the time of King Edward the Confessor, by the noble widow Rychold. The chapel had certainly been built long before it became prominent in the mid 13th century as the resort of royal and aristocratic pilgrims, but there is absolutely no evidence for a pre-Conquest foundation. The author of the ballad was simply attempting to emphasise the antiquity of the shrine by placing its origins before the great watershed in English history, the time beyond which the memory of man did not run. Many religious institutions sought in this way to enhance their status - most notably, the monks of Glastonbury had claimed that their house had been founded by Joseph of Arimathea.[2]

The founder of the chapel was, in fact, Richelde de Faverches, or de Fervaques, as stated in the charter issued by her son Geoffrey to record his establishment of a religious community at Walsingham:

> Be it known that I have given and conceded to God and St. Mary, and to Edwin my clerk, for the religious order which he shall cause to be established, the chapel which my mother founded at Walsingham in perpetual honour of the Virgin Mary, together with the church of All Saints in the same vill, with all its appurtenances…

The toponymic is clearly Norman or French rather than English or Scandinavian.[3] The widow of a Geoffrey de Fervaques occurs in the Great Roll of the Exchequer for 1130-1, which records that William of Houghton paid the Crown ten marks to have her in marriage, with custody of her son until he should reach the age of majority. This son is surely the same Geoffrey (II) de Fervaques who founded the Priory, and the charter announcing that foundation can be dated within the limits 1152 to 1156. It is possible that Richelde established the chapel on the same site shortly before 1131, when widowed from Geoffrey (I), but it is more likely that the chapel which gradually acquired the status of a shrine was founded rather later, in the late 1140s or early 1150s, when she had been widowed a second time, and after her son had visited the Holy Land.

Marian Devotion in the Early Twelfth Century

In Western Europe from the end of the 11th century there was a great upsurge of interest in and devotion to the Blessed Virgin Mary, who now rose to new prominence in the Catholic perception of the economy of salvation. This is certainly associated with the novel emphasis on the human Jesus, launched into the world to be a friend and a comfort to believers, which now complemented the earlier medieval image of the dreadful judge portrayed over the west door of so many Romanesque churches.[4] It is quite natural that this focus on the humanity of God should lead to increasing veneration of His mother. At the highest level of spirituality, this new Marian devotion was expressed in the prayers and meditations of St. Anselm, Abbot of Bec in Normandy and subsequently Archbishop of Canterbury (d. 1109). Among the populace in general, the use of the Hail Mary spread rapidly during the 12th century, and simple wooden statues of the Virgin and Child proliferated in small local churches.[5] A local manifestation of this new preoccupation, at a very high level, is provided by Bishop Herbert de Losinga (d. 1119), the founder of Norwich cathedral, who spoke extensively of her in his sermons, and who described himself as a "pious client of the Mother of God".

A particular manifestation of the cult of Mary in England was the composition of collections of her miracles.[6] A profusion of miracle collections appeared in the Anglo-Norman kingdom in the two generations after the Conquest, in contrast to the almost complete absence of these before 1066. The reason was that the properties and privileges of the Old English monasteries were under threat from the new French aristocracy, a colonial elite eager to ridicule Anglo-Saxon saints of whom they had never heard and whose names they found ridiculous and barbarous, in order to undermine the title of communities founded by or dedicated to them. There was a desperate need in the ancient monasteries of the kingdom, the last refuges of pre-Conquest culture, to accumulate and document evidence of these saints' miracles, in order to prove their authenticity and thus corroborate title deeds. Many English monasteries, however, were dedicated to St. Mary and certainly, quite apart from the rising tide of devotion to Mary, the recitation of the wonders worked by God through her could do no harm in deterring aggression against native monasteries which were especially hers. The best example is Evesham in Worcestershire, dedicated to St. Mary and St. Ecgwin. Dominic, Prior and historian of the house, did the best he could with Ecgwin, and Dominic therefore collected as many miracles of the Virgin as he could find; it was a universal collection, in which only one very undramatic miracle was associated specifically with Evesham. Another collection was produced by the more famous William of Malmesbury (d. 1143), often regarded as the founder of the historical profession in England. These English compilations have been seen as one of this island's distinctive contributions to the great flowering of learning which we conventionally call "the 12th century renaissance". They formed the basis of every western European collection of the Miracles of the Virgin throughout the rest of the Middle Ages, and their appeal to the French-speaking upper classes of 12th century England is demonstrated by the production around mid-century of a compendium of the stories in that language.

Within this general context, the third, but perhaps even the earliest, of these innovative collections of Marian miracles was compiled by Anselm of St. Saba, nephew of St. Anselm and himself Abbot of Bury St. Edmunds from 1121-48, and one of the foremost advocates of the feast of the Conception of the Blessed Virgin Mary, which having been observed in the Old English church had been eclipsed after the Conquest, but was officially restored to the calendar by a legatine council in 1129. With Abbot Anselm there is even the possibility of a close influence of Richelde de Fervaques, as there was much interaction between the two adjacent feudal honours of St. Edmunds Abbey and of the lords of Clare, of whom the Fervaques family were tenants. A later Abbot of Bury, Samson (d. 1211), is known to have preached to the people in the vernacular. It is unlikely that Anselm could do this, but it is not impossible that he did preach to aristocratic audiences in French, although perhaps more likely that his enthusiasm was communicated by his Bury monks.

These early miracle collections did not restrict the Blessed Virgin to one location, but her cult was not entirely literary, and there was an increasing tendency to appropriate her to a particular community and institution. The years around 1100 appear to mark a turning point with regard to Marian relics.[7] Before then bodily relics were practically unknown - the canons of Coutances in western Normandy were extremely dubious when their Bishop, Geoffrey (d. 1110), claimed to have discovered some of her hairs in the Cathedral. After the Christian capture of Jerusalem by the crusaders in 1099, however, a Norman crusader, Ilger de Bigod (a member of a family which settled in East Anglia and in the 1140s acquired the Earldom of Norfolk), apparently found a packet of the Virgin's hairs in the Holy Sepulchre. He brought them back home, and they were distributed among several monasteries, including the Norman house of Bec, of which the Clares, lords of the Fervaques, were conspicuous patrons. Such hair was one of the most precious relics of the Cathedral church of Laon which in 1113, following the destruction of the Cathedral by fire, were taken on a fund-raising tour on this side of the Channel. They did not get to East Anglia, but there were miracles at Dover and at Canterbury, and the Clares held extensive estates in Kent centred on Tonbridge. Again it is possible, but pure hypothesis, that news of these relics and the miracles which they wrought may have percolated through to the young Richelde. It is equally possible, but again entirely speculative, that the daughter house of Bec established by the Clare family first at their eponymous castle in Suffolk, and subsequently moved to Stoke by Clare, may have had Marian relics brought over from the mother house. We certainly have evidence of the interchange of relics between Bec and another English daughter house at St. Neots in Huntingdonshire. And it is quite certain that the relics of Stoke by Clare were sent on tour around the founder's estates - Earl Roger (1152-73) requested those who encountered them, and ordered his own men, to treat them with benevolence and generosity, in the sure hope that God would reward one-hundredfold in the next life anyone who contributed to the building work just commenced at the Priory.

There are several examples of localised Norman cults of the Blessed Virgin, which in the cosmopolitan cross-Channel world of the early 12th century would have been well known to the knightly class of colonial England. At Coutances, despite the canons' initial scepticism about bodily relics of Mary, there was by mid-century certainty as to the power of the miracle-working statue of the Virgin. The compiler of the miracle collection was quite convinced of the peculiar efficacy of St. Mary of Coutances. He told the story of a certain Vitalis, who came to the "insipid conclusion" that the Virgins of Coutances and Bayeux were the same person, that is, the mother of God, and that consequently the Virgin of Coutances could not possibly be more merciful or more powerful than the Virgin of Bayeux. He refused to accompany his fellow villagers on pilgrimage to Coutances, for which dereliction the Virgin of that cathedral severely chastised him.

In 1147 there began a great rebuilding programme at the monastery of Our Lady at St. Pierre sur Dives, which some years before had been severely damaged by fire. The reconstruction was apparently inspired by the first rebuilding of Chartres the previous year. Miracles were reported by one of the monks, Hamo, in a letter to St. Pierre's daughter house of Tutbury, Staffordshire - and the greatest miracle was the fervour with which people of all classes threw themselves into the work. There were many "cart miracles" - cures of sick people brought to the monastery on the carts containing the building materials, and these significantly included people who had failed to find a cure at Chartres. One Bayeux woman, for example, had lain at Chartres for fifteen days, and was only cured when brought to St. Pierre sur Dives - clear evidence of the superiority of the Virgin of St. Pierre to those of the two cathedral cities.

There is one further reason for the multiplication of Marian shrines and Marian miracles in this period - the continuous outbreaks of ergotism in the late 11th and early 12th centuries. This was known as *ignis sacer*, holy fire, and was caused by rye infected by a certain fungus, breaking out after wet summers. It was a horrible disease, the symptoms of which included severe gangrene, convulsions and nervous disorders. The most serious epidemics occurred in France and England in the first half of the 12th century, and almost every outbreak led to a mass pilgrimage to Marian shrines, for example, to Soissons in 1128, to Chartres in 1132. As the Soissons commentator wrote:

> ... when no human remedy could be found ... the sick, even as the fire raged within them, took refuge in the benevolence and healing power of the ever-Virgin mother of God, and she did not disappoint them in their hopes.

The Crusading Ethos

Geoffrey de Fervaques stated in his foundation charter that he had been to the Holy Land. After the Christian Conquest of Jerusalem in 1099 as the culmination of the First Crusade, access to the holy places associated with Christ's earthly life had become far easier for pilgrims, armed and otherwise. Reports were brought to the West of the various sacred sites and, in the early 12th century, buildings in Palestine became architectural models for western European churches. The military orders, the Templars and the Hospitallers, constructed their churches with round naves, in imitation of the Church of the Holy Sepulchre - the best known extant example is the Temple Church, off Fleet Street in London.[8] Such replication provides an architectural context for the imitation, however inaccurate, in Norfolk of a revered religious site, the house of the Annunciation at Nazareth.

It is very possible that Geoffrey's visit to Palestine had been as a combatant on the Second Crusade, preached by the Pope in 1144 as a response to the Moslem reconquest of Edessa and setting out in 1147.[9] This expedition, in contrast to the First Crusade, evoked widespread response in England, and there was a large East Anglian contingent, led by Hervey de Glanville and by William, Earl Warenne, who before his departure obtained the dedication of the rebuilt Priory church at Castle Acre. One known participant was a younger son of the Clare family, Geoffrey's overlords, while we have the record of a loan raised against security from St. Benet's Abbey by Philip Basset of Postwick, a lesser Norfolk lord of much the same social status as Geoffrey, so that he might finance his expedition. The East Anglian crusaders in fact achieved a spectacular success before they even reached the Holy Land, as on their way by sea they diverted to capture the city of Lisbon from the Moors, and were thus instrumental in the creation of the Christian kingdom of Portugal. Geoffrey may have been there; but in a sense this is peripheral, for the great, numbered, crusades were only highpoints in the constant coming and going to the Holy Land in the 12th century, which did much to shape the spirituality of the age. Certainly the Norman chronicler Robert de Torigni described the 1140s as a time of increasing humility, penance and contrition in the Anglo-Norman world.

The Region

In the Middle Ages East Anglia was certainly not the economically backward area which it became after the Industrial Revolution, and was no rural backwater. The Domesday Book in 1086 and the lay subsidy returns of 1334 both demonstrate it to have been the richest region of England, and to this day the hundreds of magnificent Perpendicular churches are testimony to the wealth, as well as the piety, of its inhabitants in the century and a half before the Reformation. It is traditionally believed that this wealth was based on wool and cloth, and in large part it was, although there is more to it than this. In the 12th century Dunwich, on the Suffolk coast and in the later Middle Ages destroyed by erosion, was a great port; and Bishop's (now King's) Lynn in north-west Norfolk had recently been founded as a new town with a great future. A whole string of not-so-minor ports stretched between - places like Blakeney and Cley next the Sea, now frequented mainly for sailing holidays or bird watching. Norwich was rivalled only by Bristol and York as the second city of the kingdom. Yarmouth's own fishing fleet was during the herring season swelled by a vast number of vessels from all over England and the North Sea countries. The Broads were being dug out in the 12th century to provide turves for fuel and to smoke the herrings, and salt production was being increased all along the coast to preserve them in another way. East Anglia, indeed, has recently been presented as a paradigm of the flourishing western European economy of this age, which provided a surplus for extensive religious endowment.[10]

The region had its own saints. Although Ely lies just outside its borders, St. Etheldreda's monastery had extensive estates in Suffolk. Here, however, the dominant force in terms of religion, lordship and economy was St. Edmund, the archetypal royal martyr who ruled posthumously from his borough. Norfolk was not so fortunate, and although the two counties did constitute a region, sharing the same bishop and the same royal sheriff, they did, and still do, have distinct identities - the people of Bury St. Edmunds could hardly understand Abbot Samson when he preached to them in the vernacular because of his Norfolk accent. The desperate need for a local Norfolk saint is revealed by the distressing story of little St. William of Norwich, alleged to have been ritually murdered by the Jews, in mockery of Christ's Passion, just at the time that the Second Crusade was being preached.[11] Moreover, at a time when the cult of Mary was becoming localised and appropriated by individual churches, each with its own Virgin, Norfolk and East Anglia as a whole needed its own Marian shrine.

The religious landscape of East Anglia was undergoing a transformation in the 12th century. One aspect of this was the 'parochialisation' of the church, the establishment of a local church for every village community. This was not a result of the Norman Conquest, but was a process which had begun c.900 AD, which the Domesday Book indicates to have by 1086 progressed at more rapid rate than elsewhere in England, and which was almost complete by 1200 AD.[12] More dramatic was the monastic revolution which occurred in East Anglia in the wake of the Conquest. Monastic life had been entirely eliminated by the Danish invasions of the 9th century, and before 1066 recovery had been only partial. There were in 1066 only three communities in this large region - St. Benet of Holme and Bury St. Edmunds, refounded and re-endowed by King Cnut in 1019-20, and St. Benet's cell of Rumburgh in Suffolk. This was very sparse in comparison with the heavy monastic settlement of Wessex. The situation was completely transformed in the half-century after the Conquest.[13] The new Norman lords were anxious for both the prestige and the hope of salvation conferred by patronage of Benedictine monks, who were universally regarded as the 'knights' or 'athletes' of Christ, front-line troops in the battle against Satan, armed with their elaborate liturgy offered especially for the spiritual health of their founders and benefactors. According to English custom (one of the few of which the Normans approved) the cathedral of East Anglia was relocated in Norwich in 1096 as a Benedictine community; and between c. 1080 and 1107 the great feudal families of the region founded houses of Black monks on their estates to serve as 'fortresses of prayer' - Eye and Clare in Suffolk, Castle Acre, Binham, Horsham St. Faith, Thetford and Wymondham in Norfolk. Of these seven, five were dedicated to the Blessed Virgin Mary, including the Valognes foundation of Binham, very close to Walsingham. After about 1120 fashions changed, new religious orders rose to popularity, but the lavish process of endowment continued. By 1200 AD there were over eighty monastic institutions in the diocese, over half of them fully conventual.

The Augustinian Canons

Geoffrey de Fervaques in the 1150s chose to endow, as custodians of his mother's chapel, a community of Augustinian canons, an order which, although it followed the Rule of St. Augustine, the famous 5th century bishop of Hippo, was of fairly recent origins, a product of the great papal reform movement of the late 11th century.[14] This papal reform ultimately involved the bishops of Rome in ideological conflict with the Holy Roman Emperor and other European kings over the location of authority within Christian society, but it had originated as a campaign to purge the clerical order of the great evils, as they were then newly perceived, of simony (trading in church livings), clerical marriage and hereditary succession of priests to their father's livings, and to evade the snares of the world in general. In 1059 a papal council authorised the adoption of a common rule for clergy who, although not monks, wished to live in communities. By 1100 groups of priests all over Western Europe had gathered together to live this common, canonical life, and St. Augustine's Rule, rather than giving them inspiration, provided them with respectable, antique antecedents in the writings of one of the greatest of the Fathers of the Church. The canonical movement reached England around the turn of the 11th and 12th centuries. The earliest communities, before there was an order in any real sense, were at St. Gregory's, Canterbury, St. Botolph's, Colchester, and Huntingdon. There was a marked rise in the number of foundations from 1100 to 1120, and from 1120 to 1135 an explosion, probably largely because of the favour and patronage of King Henry I, his first queen Matilda and the court circle.

In East Anglia the great families who had hitherto founded Benedictine monasteries had by the 1140s also established Augustinian communities - Bigod at Pentney, Warenne at Thetford, d'Albini at Old Buckenham. The most interesting house, however, is probably the earliest, West Acre, founded by Roger de Tosny soon after 1102. The recently rediscovered foundation charter reveals clearly two things: first, that the inspiration of the canonical movement was the life of the early church as illustrated in the Acts of the Apostles - the charter unambiguously cites the early Christian community as an exemplar; and secondly, that these early convents might have very informal beginnings - at West Acre a priest, his son and two others took an oath to observe this new, pure, priestly life and were established practically in their lord's back garden.[15] This economy of scale meant that by mid-century the knightly class, the squirearchy of the age, could join great lords as the founders of Augustinian communities - they were cheap to establish, and unlike the Benedictines they looked outwards, serving parish churches, and often having hospitals annexed to their houses, as most famously at St. Bartholomew's in London. This is the context of Geoffrey de Fervaques foundation at Walsingham. He gave the chapel dedicated to St. Mary which his mother had built to his clerk Edwin with his companions for the establishment of the life of a religious order; the charter of his lord, Roger de Clare, a few years later refers to *his* clerks of Walsingham, Ralph and Geoffrey. It was certainly initially a very small establishment, which originated in the commitment of a handful of priests to live a celibate life in a society in which the vast majority of parish clergy remained married, and in the enthusiasm of the local lord of the manor, whose father had forty years before given his tithes at Walsingham to the Benedictine monastery of Clare.

The Growth of the Priory

There are no sources available to indicate the number of canons at Walsingham for the first two centuries of its existence.[16] It is not until 1371 that we have the figure, from tax returns, of twenty religious, and we can guess with confidence that this figure had been reached, and probably surpassed, before the Black Death of 1348. Such a community is likely to have maintained about 100 retainers and servants, including their wives, either part- or full-time; so the Priory was a substantial employer, and consumer, in the locality. These figures were maintained to the end - the number of canons at visitations between 1494 and 1532 varies between 17 and 24, and in 1526 and 1532 there was a higher proportion of novices than might be expected (six and four respectively), which demonstrates that the Priory was continuing to attract entrants to the eve of the Dissolution.

Apart from anything else, the Augustinian Priory was, like all monasteries of any size, a business enterprise, and the acquisition and exploitation of resources was vital to support the canons' functions of dignified liturgical observance and hospitality. It is difficult to say a great deal about the development of the Priory estate, because the cartulary, the register of deeds granting lands and rents to the canons, has not yet been edited.[17] From it we do have in print the Bishop of Norwich's confirmation charter of c. 1200 AD, which shows the Priory by then to have received grants from Roger Clare, the founder's lord, from William, the younger brother of King Henry II, and from several knightly tenants of the Clares. This marked some improvement on the original endowment, if we can believe a late medieval note in the cartulary which states that the canons had at the beginning revenues of no more than ten marks (£6.66) *per annum*, apart from offerings at the chapel. A list of possessions of the mid 13th century details the churches of All Saints, Great Walsingham, and All Saints, Little Walsingham, £1 *p.a.* from the mill of Little Walsingham, and small parcels of land and rents in neighbouring market towns and villages such as the Snorings, Burnham Norton, Wells and Warham. The endowment gradually increased in the course of the 13th century. The canons received the churches of Bedingham, Burnham Norton and Oulton, from which they sought to maximise their revenues, and they doubtless made some profit from administering tithes granted to Stoke by Clare and Wymondham Priories and the half of Holkham church which had been given to the Abbey of Viterbo in Italy. In 1291, when the income of the English church was assessed for the purposes of papal taxation, the Walsingham Priory estate, including its parish churches, was listed at £79. Nearby West Acre was assessed at £140, Butley in Suffolk at £195. There was, however, also a note of the estimated £20 *p.a.* which was offered at the shrine of Our Lady, and this was a pointer to the future.

The financial status of Walsingham was vastly different on the eve of the Dissolution, when the gross annual income of the house was assessed by Henry VIII's commissioners in 1535 at £707, this representing £652 net after fixed charges on the revenues. Offerings were now calculated at £260, but that left £445 from the estate - £385 from land and rent, £60 from parish churches.

It was the huge sums received at the shrine which provided the capital to extend the estate, for later medieval acquisitions were largely purchases rather than gifts. The Priory paid the very heavy fines of a hundred marks (£66.66) in 1425 and £100 in 1448, plus three lesser sums later in the century, just for royal licences permitting the Canons to acquire additional estates; a list in the cartulary details the property purchased by Prior John Farewell (1474-1503) for the enormous sum of £717. By the early 16th century Walsingham had overtaken houses far better endowed in 1291 to become easily the wealthiest Augustinian house in East Anglia. The increase in estimated revenue between the two surveys, ignoring inflation, was at Walsingham a staggering 458%, while at the Augustinian Priories of Butley, West Acre and Pentney it was, respectively, 63%, 91% and 150%. Further evidence of the financial importance of the shrine in financial terms is provided by a comparison of receipts of £260 at Walsingham with estimates from other important pilgrimage centres: £36 at St. Thomas of Canterbury, £10 at the Holy Blood of Hailes, £6 only at the Holy Rood of Bromholm. There could be no surer testimony to the supremacy of Walsingham as the most popular shrine in England on the eve of the Reformation.

The Development of the Walsingham Pilgrimage

There is no evidence for pilgrimage to the Shrine for the first 70 years of the Priory's existence, until in 1226 King Henry III visited both Walsingham and the Holy Rood at Bromholm, recently acquired by the monks of that house from the loot of the sack of Constantinople in 1204. It is highly unlikely that the young king would have gone for the good of his soul to Walsingham had it not already acquired a reputation as a pilgrimage centre. Indeed, around this time the hospital of Beck at Billingford was founded by William de Bec for the nightly reception of thirteen pilgrims on the road from Norwich to Walsingham. In 1226 King Henry granted the canons an annual fair and a weekly market, which would provide them with a continual source of revenue. Until 1256 the king made regular visits, usually marked by substantial gifts, most notably in 1246 a golden crown for the image of St. Mary. This is significant as it suggests that, although the Holy House was preserved within the Priory church until the Reformation, the chief object of veneration had by the mid 13th century become the statue of the Virgin and Child. The late medieval Priory seal shows a representation of this, from which it appears to have been of late 12th century style, and to have borne a close resemblance to Our Lady of Rocamadour in Quercy, to which King Henry II had felt great devotion.

Henry III's royal successors imitated his pilgrimages to Walsingham. Edward I was apparently initially prompted when, while playing chess, he narrowly escaped death from a stone falling from the roof. Thereafter he made twelve recorded visits, and in 1296 concluded there a treaty with the Count of Flanders. Almost every king thereafter upto the Reformation came as a pilgrim, and their gifts continued to flow. Edward I offered a gilded silver statue of himself; his successors were rather less ostentatious, often giving gold brooches. The English aristocracy, and from the second half of the 14th century noble foreign visitors, were scarcely less generous. In 1381, for example, the Earl of Suffolk bequeathed a silver statue of a mounted knight bearing his arms, and in 1433 the Bishop of Worcester willed to the Shrine a selection of the relics which he had acquired in Rome. John Capgrave, Prior of the Augustinian friars of Lynn (d. 1464), quoting from the lost annals of the shrine, lists other gifts, notably a picture of the Annunciation set with precious stones given by Henry Earl of Lancaster (d. 1345) and valued at 400 marks (£266), and vessels to the same value given by his son Duke Henry (d. 1361). We must imagine the statue of the Virgin and Child, and that of St. Gabriel which stood beside it in the chapel from the late 13th century at the latest, surrounded by a plethora of splendid treasures, but also by a multitude of lesser offerings: images in wax of shrivelled limbs which had been cured, even of whole bodies, as the wax image of the weight of his body given by John Paston's mother-in-law when he was sick; and wax images, too, of ships offered by sailors such as those saved in 1343 from drowning by their prayers to Our Lady of Walsingham and St. Edmund.

The popularity of the shrine amongst those who would never have been honourably received in the guest-house of the Priory is obliquely revealed by the canons' opposition in 1346 to the establishment of a Franciscan Friary in the town, partly on the grounds that pilgrims received there would represent a security risk to the treasures in their custody; and also by the arson allegedly committed by pilgrims in 1431 at four local inns whose landlords were regarded as profiteers. The criticism levelled particularly at Walsingham both by orthodox reformers and by Lollard heretics is also an indication of the shrine's pulling power. In 1346 the great preacher Archbishop FitzRalph of Armagh gently warned that the cult might distract hearts and minds from true contemplative religion, while the poet of Piers Plowman had his character of Avarice going on a hypocritical pilgrimage to Bromholm and Walsingham. Lollard writers at about the same time derided "Falsingham" and "the witch of Walsingham". In the early 16th century the Christian humanist Desiderius Erasmus visited Walsingham and penned his famous denigration of the shrine and its custodians, in which he expressed totally unrealistic expectations of the canons' learning and a supercilious contempt for manifestations of popular religion and for relics which, if they did no physical good, certainly caused no spiritual or mental harm.

Despite such criticism from the intellectual elite and from a tiny alienated minority of heretics, the popularity of Walsingham continued unabated to the very eve of the English Reformation. Henry VII prayed there in 1487 before battle, and after his victory over the adherents of Lambert Simnel at Stoke sent his battle standard as an offering; thereafter he made three further pilgrimages. His son, who was eventually to destroy Walsingham and so many other shrines, in his early years displayed no doubts. Soon after his accession Henry VIII made the final stage of his journey, from Barsham, barefoot, and gave a necklace of great value. In 1511 he paid for the royal glazier to reglaze the Lady Chapel. His wife, Katherine of Aragon, made the pilgrimage in 1513 as a thanks-offering for his victory over the Scots at Flodden, and again in 1517, perhaps to pray for the safe delivery of a male heir. In 1524 Cardinal Wolsey obtained from Rome a plenary indulgence for the king and twenty others who might make an annual pilgrimage to Walsingham, Bury St. Edmunds or Canterbury. To the very end, there is evidence too, from wills, of continuing devotion and benefactions to Our Lady of Walsingham, from the court circle down to quite humble testators.[18]

The Late Medieval Priory

It is in the nature of late medieval governmental records, both of the English state and of the church, that religious houses featured therein most commonly when something was amiss, when there was a jurisdictional dispute or internal dissent, and that normal, regular observance went unremarked. Prior John Snoring (1374-1401) was almost continually involved in litigation, but this stemmed from his laudable ambition to increase the status of his house. He engaged in a large-scale building programme, which stretched the Priory's resources, and worked to have Walsingham elevated to abbatial status, and perhaps also to have the community exempted from the authority of the Bishop of Norwich. The incumbent of the see, Henry Despencer (1370-1406), was a vehement defender of every privilege of his office, and invoked royal power to frustrate any appeal by the Prior to Rome before deposing him from office in 1389. Snoring was now permitted by the English government to appeal to the Pope, and was restored. He then fought another case at the papal court for exemption from visitation fees due to the bishop. He was finally removed from office by the Archbishop of Canterbury during his visitation of 1401, but was awarded a comfortable pension for his retirement. Such disputes concerning status and jurisdiction were the commonplace of medieval ecclesiastical politics, and do not reflect at all on the religious observance of the community. Had he succeeded, Snoring would have been regarded at Walsingham as a hero who had secured the rights of the Priory and of its heavenly patron.

The evidence from the 50 years before the Dissolution is apparently more damaging, since it concerns the internal life of the house. Five times between 1494 and 1532 the Priory was formally visited by the Bishop of Norwich or his commissioners.[19] They, of course, were intent on detecting and correcting any abuses. Laudable observance in monasteries was dismissed simply with the words "all well", and this entry has all too often been interpreted by modern historians as evidence of a successful conspiracy to disguise the truth by complicity in false testimony, while the witness of brethren disgruntled with their superior and eager to find fault has been taken at face value. Because of the peculiar status of the shrine particular attention has been focused on the Walsingham visitations, and they have been cited as an example of the decline of the communal religious life throughout England as a whole. It is doubtful if they will bear this weight. In 1494 the faults detected were fairly trivial - some canons accused the Prior of partiality, and he had failed to produce satisfactory accounts. The situation in 1514 was very much more serious. The Prior was now William Lowthe, a client of Henry VII's notorious ministers Empson and Dudley, who had been intruded into headship ten years before. The visitor found a community riven by faction, and a Prior who was accused of embezzling offerings from the shrine and treating some of the community's lands as his own, and moreover of having as his mistress the wife of one of the Priory servants who himself intimidated the canons. It is difficult to know just how much of this was true, as the Priory was divided into competing factions. Against the conclusion of terminal decline which has been based on these charges, various points must be made: that any community of men or women living in close proximity is likely to be subject periodically to such strains; that no visitation records survive from the supposed "golden age" of the 12th and 13th centuries, although other sources reveal occasional scandals just as bad as any on the eve of the Dissolution; and that indiscipline was an internal matter, which certainly did not detract from the popularity of the shrine (although it should be noted that Erasmus penned his criticisms at this time). Most importantly, something decisive was done - the Prior was compelled to resign. The visitation return of 1520 reveals a new Prior struggling to restore discipline, although, as might be expected, meeting with opposition from a group of alienated brethren. By 1526 the situation was once more reasonably satisfactory. These records reveal, therefore, a temporary breakdown of discipline, but also that the regulatory procedures of the medieval church were effective.

The End

After Henry VIII's rapid change of heart resulting from his matrimonial problems, Walsingham suffered the common fate of all the religious houses of England. On 18th September 1534 the Prior and 21 canons sealed and signed a deed accepting the king as head of the English church and renouncing papal authority. In 1535 the Valor Ecclesiasticus provided for the crown an assessment of the rich pickings potentially available from the monasteries, and about the same time an enquiry was conducted into alleged miracles at Walsingham and the origin of the Holy House, the statue and the Virgin's milk - this appears to have been based on Erasmus' partial account, which fitted the bill perfectly for the government. In 1536 royal injunctions launched the national campaign against images, but a month before this, although Walsingham was certainly not one of the smaller houses to be dissolved in 1536, it was reported to Thomas Cromwell, the king's chief minister, that all jewels, plate and money found there had been confiscated. A royal visitation was conducted, and the commissioners denounced not only the immorality of some of the canons, but also pretended relics and miracles. Throughout all these proceedings, pilgrims continued to come to the shrine.

As rumours of impending dissolution spread, there was much local discontent, in part certainly because of heavy economic dependence on the Priory and on pilgrims. In April 1537 a plot for insurrection was hatched at nearby Binham, but the conspirators were betrayed to the government, and on 30th May twelve persons, including the subprior of Walsingham, were executed.

In July 1538 the statue of the Blessed Virgin, with the valuables still left around it, was carried off to London and was destroyed at Chelsea, along with Our Lady of Ipswich. The Prior of Walsingham was still hoping against hope for the survival of his house, petitioning for its conversion into a college of secular priests; but on 4th August 1538 the Priory was surrendered to the Crown. Most of the canons received either parochial livings or pensions. In November 1539 Thomas Sydney of Little Walsingham purchased the site of the monastery.

It is now appreciated by historians, as it was not until relatively recently, that the English Reformation was not eagerly embraced by the vast majority of the English people, on whom it was in fact foisted by a small group of Protestant courtiers and divines at the centre of power in London.[20] It was enforced by a campaign of terror. The huge investment in traditional religion right up to the break with Rome was channelled largely into parish churches, of which East Anglia has so many fine late medieval examples. The monasteries which had dominated the religious life of the 12th and 13th centuries had been eclipsed in popular affection, if not in economic status. Yet there was still a need for peculiarly sacred sites which transcended the boundaries of the parish, and even of the shire. Walsingham fulfilled this need at the close of the Middle Ages, in the age of strong parochial loyalties, just as it had earlier in a religious world dominated by monks and friars. To the end it provided a goal, both physical and spiritual, for all levels of English society, and thus it represented an ideal of religious and social unity which was shattered by the cataclysm of the Henrician Reformation.

REFERENCES

These have been kept to a minimum, and are designed to guide readers to major works which set Walsingham in the wider context of medieval religion.

1. The ballad is printed in J. C. Dickinson, The Shrine of Our Lady of Walsingham, Cambridge (1956) p.124-30. This book is the standard account of the shrine and the Priory, and this paper is heavily dependent upon it for details of Walsingham's history.
2. R. F. Treharne, The Glastonbury Legends, London (1967) esp. p.30-1.
3. L. C. Loyd, "The Origin of Some Anglo-Norman Families," Harliean Society Vol. CIII, (1951) p.41. Fervaques, Calvados, arr. Lisieux, cant. Livarot.
4. C. Morris, The Discovery of the Individual, 1050-1200, London (1972) esp. p.23-5, p.118-20, p.163-4.
5. C. Morris, The Papal Monarchy: the Western Church from 1050 to 1250, Oxford, (1989) p.302, p.377, p.464-5; for the growth of Marian pilgrimage, R. C. Finucane, Miracles and Pilgrims: Popular Beliefs in Medieval England, London (1977) p.196-9.
6. R. W. Southern, "The Place of England in the Twelfth-Century Renaissance", in his Medieval Humanism and Other Studies, Oxford (1970) p.172-4; B. Ward, Miracles and the Medieval Mind, Aldershot (1982) ch. 8.
7. For local cults of the Virgin, see J. Sumption, Pilgrimage: an Image of Medieval Religion, London (1975) p.49-51.
8. C. Brooke and W. Swaan, The Monastic World, London (1974) p.163-6.
9. C. Tyerman, England and the Crusades, 1095-1588, Chicago (1988) p.32-5.

10. See the Creighton Lecture by James Campbell, shortly to be published (UEA, Norwich) as Herring, Peat and Salt: Eastern East Anglia as a Focus of Early Modern Economic Growth.
11. For brief notices of St. Edmund and St. William, see D. H. Farmer, The Oxford Dictionary of Saints, Oxford (1978) p.120-2, p.405.
12. J. Blair, ed., Ministers and Parish Churches: the Local Church in Transition, 950-1200, Oxford University Committee for Archaeology, Monograph 17 (1988) p.1-20, p.179-90.
13. For a synopsis, see I. Atherton et al., eds, Norwich Cathedral: Church, City and Diocese, 1096-1996, London (1996) ch. 14.
14. The basic study is J. C. Dickinson, The Origins of the Austin Canons and their Introduction into England, London (1950); see also J. Burton, Monastic and Religious Orders in England, 1000-1300, Cambridge (1994) ch. 3.
15. I owe this example to Dr. Nicholas Vincent, who rediscovered the West Acre foundation charter.
16. What follows is based largely on Dickinson, The Shrine of Our Lady of Walsingham.
17. The manuscript is British Library, ms. Cotton Nero E vii.
18. For the conservation of early 16th century wills in general, see J. J. Scarisbrick, The Reformation and the English People, Oxford (1984) ch. 1.
19. For the Latin text of the visitations, see A. Jessopp, ed., Visitations of the Diocese of Norwich, A.D. 1492-1532, Camden Society n.s. 43 (1888) p.57-60, p.113-23, p.147-8, p.170-2, p.252-3, p.314-5; for discussion, D. Knowles, The Religious Orders in England iii, Cambridge (1959), p.73-5.
20. See especially E. Duffy, The Stripping of the Altars: Traditional Religion in England, 1400-1580, Yale (1992); C. Haigh, English Reformations: Religion, Politics and Society under the Tudors, Oxford (1993); C. Harper-Bill, The Pre-Reformation Church in England, 1400-1530, London (1989); Scarisbrick, op. cit.; R. N. Swanson, Church and Society in Late Medieval England, Oxford (1989); J. A. F. Thomson, The Early Tudor Church and Society, 1485-1529, London (1993).

REMEMBRANCE OF THE SHRINE 1538 - 1897

by Rev. William M McLoughlin, OSM

On coming to prepare this paper for the Centenary Historical Conference, drawing on my as yet unpublished doctoral research material, it became clear that the span was perhaps unmanageable and could result in a vast and tedious array of facts and dates. It seemed to warrant a preface with a brief point about how one is engaging in history in such a paper. It has been said that the past does not exist. What we call the past is our present thinking about what went on before us. Today the past is changing with incredible rapidity because our ways of thinking are in flux and expansion. It seems that this point is well demonstrated in any study of Walsingham: there is this tension between the fact that the past does not exist and yet the past happened.

To be immediately provocative, one must ask **what** in fact has been restored at Walsingham and **why** as a result of an interval of centuries during which there was a remembrance? What expectations were there in this intervening period from destruction to restoration and to what did they give rise? There is no doubt that great attention has been given to original sites, authentic re-creation of symbols of devotion and recovery of items associated with the original shrine and its history. But has that really been the priority? One easily answers no to this 'aunt sally' question. Has it then been simply a restoration of a pilgrimage centre after a break of four centuries. Has it been a restoration of a cult of the Blessed Virgin Mary that revives a medieval past or does it stand confidently within the living tradition that moves forward. To state the obvious, today two major focal points of devotion to Our Lady of Walsingham exist in the environs of the ancient shrine; one within Little Walsingham in the care of the Anglicans and the other at the Slipper Chapel in the care of the Roman Catholics. The establishment of these two centres occurred within a shared time span at the turn of the century, but circumstances kept them firmly separate ventures. What preceded this time in the period of remembering needs now to be understood and honestly faced. Note well, please, no reference was made to there being two shrines in separate hands, because after many years of a kind of rivalry that has been far from healthy, the spirit of the times requires us to view things in a better way. Perhaps it will be served by remembering the past afresh.

Early medieval Marian pilgrimages had continued the post-Islamic trend of replicating or "replacing" the lost shrines of Palestine and other parts of the Near East and previous speakers have spoken of the manner of the first beginnings of the Shrine at Walsingham, with its traditional date of foundation as 1061. This dating shown in the famous 21 verse Ballad, printed by Richard Pynson in 1496, is in the context of the story of the Lady Richeldis begging Our Lady to be allowed to honour her in some outstanding work. The Virgin then leads her "in spirit" to Nazareth and shows her the little house where "Gabriel her greeted" (i.e. the house of the Annunciation, then incorporated within the precincts of the Basilica of the Annunciation). There the Virgin commanded Richeldis to make another house like it at Walsingham. The Pynson Ballad clearly expresses the remembrance by a theme of reduplication "In a Memoryall of the Great Joy of my Salutacyon":

O England great cause thou hast glad for to be
compared to the Land of promise, Sion,
Thou attainest my grace to stand in that degree
Through this gracious Lady's supportacion,
To be called in every realm and region
The Holy Land, Our Lady's Dowry:
Thus art thou named of old antiquity.

And this is the cause, as it appeared by likeliness,
In thee is builded New Nazareth, a mansion
To the honour of the heavenly Empress
And of her most glorious Salutation,
When Gabriel said at Old Nazareth, "Ave"
This Joy here daily remembered to be.

The importance of this is the influence it was to have in the manner of remembering during the years from destruction to revival of the public cult. There is little doubt that in the absence of public places of Marian devotion in England, those who travelled were inevitably influenced by the sight of the shrines abroad. The pilgrimage literature abounds in reference to dimensions and measurements of holy sites. Loreto and its tradition of the physical translation of the original Holy House of Nazareth (made of stone, 32 feet long, 13 feet wide, and 18 feet high) dated at 1291 comes later than the traditional date of Walsingham's Holy House (whose dimensions are known to us through William of Worcester's later 15th century measuring showing it to be considerably smaller at 23 feet 6 inches long by 12 feet 10 inches wide and made of wood). In the early efforts to restore the cult, the Loreto dimensions influenced the Chapel at the Church of the Annunciation at King's Lynn and also the Hope Patten structure in the Anglican shrine church, in the absence at that time of awareness of the precise information about the original wooden structure, later to be confirmed in the 1961 excavation of the site. Interestingly, the dimensions of the Slipper Chapel, being 28 feet 6 inches long, and 12 feet 5 inches wide, has a closeness to the dimensions of the Loreto Holy House. From the outset, however, no claim was ever made for the Walsingham Holy House to have been anything more than a way of remembering the place and event of the Annunciation in a new Nazareth here. It also, however, explains in some measure the drivenness of those who, in the early efforts to come to Walsingham, were so focused on sites and the task of restoring a remembrance in continuity with what had been there before, that a sad adversarial stance developed.

In July 1538, under Henry VIII the Prior and Canons were forced to sign the Act of Supremacy and the Priory was suppressed. Whatever its fate, the famous image of Our Lady of Walsingham was taken away by the King's Commissioners, together with much gold and silver. Some have believed that the original image was secretly buried and may still turn up somewhere. However, it seems unlikely that a copy rather than the original was taken to London to be burnt in Chelsea together with some other highly venerated images, collected from different places of pilgrimage in the kingdom. The King took over the priory, build-

Remains of the East Window of the Priory.

ings, land and all that the canons held in trust, and sold it to individuals. The canons were pensioned off and soon the stones of the priory were dismantled. Hope Patten imaginatively described the dissolution of Walsingham: "the wealth of the pilgrims' offerings of five centuries was deposited in the King's Treasury in the Tower of London. The Holy House was destroyed, the outer Church and Priory razed to the ground, the original Holy Well desecrated and blocked with clay, the lead stripped from the roofs, the glass smashed and altars overthrown." (A. Hope Patten, England's National Shrine of Our Lady, Past and Present. Walsingham, 2nd.ed., undated)

Despite this ending of what is remembered as one of the most magnificent monasteries of medieval England, its memory lingered on and even in the days of persecution it is said that some individuals continued to go on pilgrimage to the now desecrated Walsingham Holy House. This might strengthen the claim that venerated as the image of the Virgin had most certainly been, it was the place that had served as a remembrance that still drew those who thought of the Blessed Virgin despite the absence of all else.

In 1539, a year later, a poor woman of Wells was paraded through the town for daring to claim that Our Lady of Walsingham, the Virgin Mary, still granted favours. Sir Roger Townsend wrote in his report to Cromwell "Howbeit, I cannot but perceive the seyd Image is not yett out of sum of their heddes". Not too remarkable that memory would not be so short, but remarkable in that the shock to devotees of the shrine of what had happened must have made all but the very brave continue to demonstrate that remembrance.

More discreet and continuing remembrance of Walsingham as a holy place was expressed perhaps in the presence of religious who lived in the village after the Dissolution, including the half-sister of St. John Fisher and a relative of one of the Carthusian martyrs (from Dartmouth Convent). Of their fate on the accession and later death of Mary Tudor there is as yet no discovered material.

Marian devotion was clearly and frequently to be an endangering practice but it persisted. Many conformed to the new religion, but in their hearts would have remained Catholic. A manuscript *Epiphanius in ancorato* internally dated as having been written in 1555 for a Catholic reader presents the issue of Images and their importance. In 1577 it was reported that in Essex "There be divers bold disorders and riotous assemblies of divers Papists at Colchester.....They maintaine lakyn" (i.e. devotion to Our Lady) "in great boldness.......They have got into their fellowshippe a Justice of the Peace" who "shadoweth them" (3/PRO, S.P. 12,120,No.6 Transcribed by Canon Foley, Harlow - unpublished research). In the same year two brothers, George and William Binkes, tailors of Finchingfield, were charged for William saying "What manner of religion we have here in England, I know not, for ye preachers now do preach their own inventions" and George expressing the view that "The Masse is good, that Images are good and ought to stand in the church to put men in remembrance that such saints there were..." (M. D. R. Leys, Catholics in England 1559-1829: A Social History. Longmans, Green & Co, 1961).

The issue of images was one of the rare occasions when a remembrance of Walsingham by name featured in Anglican instruction. It had a negative character and appears in *The Book of Homilies* (The Third Part of the Sermon against Peril of Idolatry. Oxford, 1802 p.188) saying: "And where one faint has images in divers places, the fame faint hath divers names thereof, most like to the Gentiles. When you hear of Our Lady of Walfingham, Our Lady of Ipfwich, Our Lady of Wilfdon and fuch others; what is it but an imitation of the Gentiles idolaters? Diana Agrotera, Diana Coriphea, Diana Ephesia, &c. Venus Cypria, Venus Paphia, Venus Gnidia. Whereby is evidently meant, that the faint for the image fake fhould in thofe places, yea, in the images themfelves have a dwelling, which is the ground of their idolatry. For where no images be, they have no such means."

By the end of the 16th century, almost 50 years after the dissolution of the priory, an anonymous poem had been written by one who still remembered and presumably had personally visited the destroyed shrine. Attributed by some to Philip Howard, Earl of Arundel, who died in the Tower of London after his return to the Catholic Faith, it expressed the bitterness and sorrow over the loss of Our Lady of Walsingham. Robert Southwell, S.J. is an alternative possible author of the poem because of his family connections with the place through the unscrupulous Richard Southwell, who was one of the King's Visitors of the Priory at the Dissolution, and through Robert's service in the Arundel household. The poem graphically describes the devastation, the "wrecks" of Walsingham, over which many must have felt deeply grieved.

In the wrecks of Walsingham
Whom should I choose
But the Queen of Walsingham
To be guide to my muse?

Then, thou Prince of Walsingham,
Grant me to frame
Bitter plaints to rue they wrong
Bitter woe for thy name

Bitter was it, O to see
The silly sheep
Murdered by the ravening wolves
While the shepherds did sleep

Bitter was it, O to view
The sacred vine
Whilst the gardeners played all close,
Rooted up by the swine

Bitter, bitter, O to behold
The grass to grow
Where the walls of Walsingham
So stately did show

Such were the worth of Walsingham
while she did stand;
Such are the wrecks as now do show
Of that holy land.

Level, level with the ground
The towers do lie,
Which, with their golden glittering tops
Pierced out to the sky.

Where were gates no gates are now,
the ways unknown
Where the press of friars did pass
While her fame far was blown

Owls do screech where the sweetest hymns
Lately were sung;
Toads and serpents hold their dens
Where the palmers did throng.

Weep, weep O Walsingham
Whose days are nights:
Blessings turned to blasphemies,
Holy deeds to despites

Sin is where Our Lady sat;
Heaven is turned to hell;
Satan sits where Our Lord did sway -
Walsingham, O farewell.

The closing line sums up the situation of Marian piety, which is denied a public expression.

Throughout the 17th and 18th centuries there was no Catholic public cultus of The Blessed Virgin Mary. From the start of Elizabeth Tudor's long reign, it had been systematically eradicated and destroyed, made actually illegal with the penalty of treason laws. Every vestige of the devotion of pre-Reformation times, when England had been the Dowry of Mary, had been done away with: shrines, images, pilgrimages, rosaries, all was gone. The devotion had been a national characteristic renowned throughout Christendom. (T. E. Bridgett, Our Lady's Dowry. London, Burns & Oates, 1875). By this stage, this was all but a memory. The nation had lost, abandoned or been deprived of all thought of Mary, for the English Reformation had been carried through by means of change in the liturgy which excluded all invocation of Mary, because of which there was a gradual fading of her from Anglican devotional life. The public worship of the nation still contained some features of actual veneration of Mary but the suppression of all invocation of Mary had eradicated the real sense and meaning of devotion to her. My Servite confrere, Fr. Gerard Corr points out that Marian Catholic devotion was therefore of necessity practised privately if at all and secretly because illegal. It was highly dangerous and could lead to the severest consequences.

Of the many questions that might be asked about the English Catholics of this time, one for us must be what expression of devotion to The Blyssed Ladye was possible for them? Seen as a silent minority who suffered with indignation rather than resignation, they were targeted for repression and gradual elimination through a series of legislative acts called the Penal Laws against Papists and Recusants. In the application of these laws a determining indication of guilt was perceived in the possession of anything which revealed devotion to the Virgin Mary, especially a rosary. The intensity and tenacity of devotion to Mary among Catholics manifested itself clearly here when many took the risk of praying the rosary privately and some suffered the consequences. The martyrdoms of St. John Almond (1612), St. John Ogilvie (1615) and others later were hallmarked by the martyrs clutching their rosaries and at the last throwing their beads to bystanders. Beads had become a dangerous identification badge of Catholics and at the scaffold the rosary was a touching proof of a persistent love of Mary. This dramatic evidence of continuing discernible Marian devotion is underpinned by other insights. A woman aged 80-90 at Highgate, who had lived through the reigns of Henry VIII, Edward VI and Mary, and then from Elizabeth's accession had conformed to the times, met Luisa de Carvajal who brought about her reconciliation to the Faith. The old woman during all that time had apparently been a Protestant but said she had never ceased to commend herself to the Virgin's protection. (G. Fullerton, Life of Luisa de Carvajal. London, 1904). In 1616 the then Archbishop of York sent pursuivants to report on devotees of Our Lady of Mount Grace gathering at the isolated shrine chapel for prayer and ordered the building to be unroofed. These few examples serve here to show the continuing existence of devotion, but our need is to know how it was expressed.

Dedication of life to the Blessed Virgin is seen in the great Mary Ward (1585-1645) of IBVM fame who saw the honour of our Blessed Lady as one of the three things for which we ought to lay down our lives and she was prepared to do so. We know of her visiting shrines of Our Lady as a pilgrim on her journeys to Rome including The Santissima Anunziata at Florence and the Holy House of Loreto, but evidence of any similar pilgrimage within England has not come to light, though there is every possibility that as a York recusant she might well have been among those who visited the chapel of Our Lady of Mount Grace at Osmotherley. Though not known to have personally pilgrimaged there, Lady Grace Fortescue, reconciled by Fr. John Gerard, about 1605, "dedicated her household and herself to the Blessed Virgin Mary of Loreto, to be her handmaid and the handmaid of her Son, offering herself and all she had for ever. As a symbol of this offering she had a heart of gold made, very finely wrought, to send to Loreto." (P. Caraman, John Gerard.

1956, p.163). These two examples show a need for a reference point for devotion that is a physical place. In the absence of England's own surviving and tolerated Marian places, it is interesting that the Annunciation reference of shrines abroad is the one followed and which attracts.

Regular and Secular Clergy coming back into the country from the seminaries and the religious houses of the still Catholic countries brought with them the lost Marian teaching, devotion and instruction that now came in fresh and vigorous form. There was an evident conviction among them that alongside the ministry of the Mass and the Sacraments, devotion to Mary was one of the most effective means of keeping Catholics together in their faith. The Jesuits in this, as so often in other things, were outstanding inspirers and organisers and they used methods of Marian devotion that had succeeded in other countries. With more express bearing on remembrance of Walsingham are the references that appeared in citation of Walsingham in the Marian Atlases that appeared throughout the latter half of the 17th century in the Jesuit writers Nieremberg (1658), Gumpenberg (1672) and Maracci (1694). Each writer remembers the devotion of Edward I for England's Nazareth because of his deliverance from being crushed by a falling piece of masonry when, without obvious reason, he felt impelled to move away from the table at which he was playing chess. This same King captured Nazareth during the Crusades in 1291 but had been unable to hold it. He was subsequently lavish in his efforts to glorify England's Nazareth. Were the Jesuit writers et al. simply dependent on each other as a source, ultimately all drawing on Thomas of Walsingham's first recounting of the miraculous deliverance of the King or independently perpetuating remembrance of Walsingham? The Provost of Northampton, Frederick Husenbeth in the late 19th century published an *Historical Calendar of Feasts of the Blessed Virgin*, which he tells us first appeared during the minority of Louis XIV of France, including every place of pilgrimage throughout Christendom. Under 28th November is the feast of Our Lady of Walsingham with the story of the deliverance of Edward I as told by Thomas of Walsingham in his *Historia Anglicana*. It is significant that in its contemporary obscurity, Walsingham is not forgotten. Similarly influential were the English religious in houses abroad, who continued contact with their families and brought to their awareness fresh devotion and reawakening of old devotion too.

Some surprise is expressed at the failure of the Austin Canons, whose Order had had the care of the Holy House of Walsingham, to promote the memory of Walsingham. It may also be that discoveries are yet to be made in archives abroad. Perhaps that is very simply explained in that the non-centralized character of this branch of the Regulars failed to produce a focus of effort to perpetuate the cult of the Lady of Walsingham. The Franciscans, in their superb Marian work on the English Mission, had to wait until the early 20th century to have an opportunity to return, but in their teaching referred often to the Dowry of Mary language that had hallmarked the cult of Walsingham.

John Wesley's only visit to Little Walsingham was on Tuesday 30th October 1781 and he wrote of it in his journal: "At two in the afternoon I preached at Walsingham, a place famous for many generations. Afterwards I walked over what is left of the famous Abbey, the east end of which is still standing. We then went to the Friary; the cloisters and chapel whereof are almost entire. Had there been a grain of virtue or public spirit in Henry the Eighth, these noble buildings need not have run to ruin." We have nothing directly on the Marian significance of the place, but know that Wesley tried ever to be at one with any with whom it was possible to find common ground as expressed in his *Letter to a Roman Catholic, 7.* His closing words at Walsingham are not surely improperly interpreted by saying he saw good in the place and regretted its destruction as he saw it.

A Methodist leaflet, given to me by Arthur Bond, introducing visitors to the 1793/94 present Walsingham Methodist chapel, which is the oldest still in use in East Anglia, recalls that since that incident of the woman of Wells, "From then until this century there were always those who quietly remained faithful to the shrine and dreamed of restoring it." This is a statement made in many forms and from many quarters. At times it might be argued that it is merely an oft repeated remark without evidence or real foundation. On the other hand, the frequency of its appearance may reflect a common experience of remembrance that at times is nostalgic and at others inspired by a continuing love and devotion. The 14th century chapel of the shrine of Our Lady of Mount Grace near Osmotherley, as mentioned earlier in this paper, escaped destruction during the Reformation and remained standing in its isolated location until it was made roofless in 1616. In the 1960's when work began on its restoration as a shrine of Our Lady, workers were surprised over the months of their labour at the frequent arrival of pilgrims, coming independently of each other and without any organisation to pray at this holy place, being, as they said, something that their families had traditionally done. Perhaps Walsingham had a similar hidden record of anonymous pilgrimage, which could not be publicised for fear of unwelcome reaction.

Much can be learnt from an institution's surviving archives and library. In the case of Walsingham, we are denied that help, which would have been a powerful influence on how it was remembered. No medieval catalogue survives and we do not know of any surviving volume that shows a press mark. This does not mean the volumes are not somewhere out there, but perhaps in an indirect way the disappearance of the holdings indicates Henry VIII's very special animus against Marian Shrines, but nowhere more so than at Walsingham itself, where he was thought to have been most disappointed. One surviving manuscript from the Priory, however, is The Chester Beatty Library Ms. 22 *Walsingham Bible*: Gen-Ruth. Thought to have been the first volume of a complete Bible, this manuscript has been connected with Walsingham because the contemporary rental of the Priory was used as a flyleaf (f.2). Its provenance shows its presence in England until its removal to Dublin where it now resides: Sir Henry Spelman (1564? - 1641), antiquary; Hon. Richard Bateman; John Jackson FSA, 1774; Sir Thomas Phillipps, Cheltenham (1792 - 1872); Sir A. Chester Beatty from Phillipps Collection 1921. Sir Henry Spelman was educated at the Grammar School at Walsingham and it seems possible that he may have acquired the manuscript during this period, although this is merely conjecture. He gives a short account of Walsingham Priory in his *Icenia* (Works, vol.ii., p.149) which includes the story of Henry VIII walking barefoot from Barsham to the Chapel of Our Lady and offering a necklace of immense value ('peringentis precii'). This image, he also tells us, was subsequently burnt at Chelsea by order of Thomas Cromwell. In his *History of Sacrilege* (4th edition, ed. C. F. S. Warren, 1895, p.146) he also tells us: "One [Thomas] Sydney, governor of the spital there, as was commonly reported when I was a scholar at Walsingham, was by the townsmen employed to have bought the site of the abbey to the use of the town, but obtained and kept it to himself."

Artefacts obviously also play a great part in remembrance and the longing to have things that establish a connection with something precious that has been lost is often great. In Bernard W. Kelly's *Historical Dictionary on English Catholic Missions* (London, Kegan Paul, Trench, Truber & Co. Ltd., 1907 p.237 - Entry under King's Lynn) it reads "Some of the candlesticks used in the church are old pre-Reformation ones from the priory of Walsingham, in the neighbourhood." As to the reliability of the provenance of these candlesticks, who can say?

The 19th century saw a development in interest in things antiquarian, and ruined ecclesiastical sites that had previously served as little more than quarries for local building, now took on new importance and fascination. Blomfield's *History of Norfolk* wrote fully about Walsingham. The Lee Warner excavations brought to light better understanding of the original shrine site, but could not provide as much as the later archaeological dig in 1961 was able to do.

Excavation of Walsingham Priory - 1961.

But these rememberings were surely not the inspiration of those whose efforts were that our Lady "may once again have a full and quiet possession of her ancient Dowry". (*An Abridgement of the rule of the Sodality of Our Blessed Lady* 1726). Waterton, Bridgett and others marshalled a tremendous account of the Marian tradition of England and along with numerous writers had kept before the attention of readers this rich tradition of the Dowry of Mary, which was to motivate so much determination. Others were perhaps more forceful in their approach. The Rev. Frederick William Faber of the London Oratory, addressing the Catholics around him in 1862, says in the preface to his translation of St. Louis Marie Grignon de Montfort's (1673-1716) *Traite de la Vraie Devotion a La Sainte Vierge* (The TDTBVM was only found in 1842): "Here in England Mary is not half enough preached. Devotion to her is low, thin and poor. It is frightened out of its wits by the sneers of heresy. It is always invoking human respect and carnal prudence, wishing to make Mary so little of a Mary that Protestants may feel at ease about her. Its ignorance of theology makes it unsubstantial and unworthy. It is not the prominent characteristic of our religion which it ought to be. It has no faith in itself." Discretion, as opposed to confident proclamation of devotion!

Inevitably, to understand the revival of interest in the shrine and of its pilgrimage there, one needs to swiftly think of the ecclesiastical scene of the 19th century. The influence of the Oxford Movement from the 1830's onwards brought about a renewed interest in Catholicity within the Anglican Church and a revival of devotion to the Blessed Virgin Mary. That influence also came to bear on the Roman Catholic community, most obviously in certain notable individuals who accepted communion with Rome. The objectives of the Oxford Movement had been to ensure Catholic practice and orthodox doctrine in the Anglican communion. Critics of the movement were to say that perhaps it was more successful in restoring the externals of Catholicism. This led to the charge that for some of the devotees of the Oxford Movement, uncritical medievalism seemed a disturbing preoccupation. John Bossey's (The English Catholic Community 1570-1850. London, Darton, Longman & Todd, 1975 p147) comment on the wider point of English Catholic practice is ad rem: "We cannot simply regard post-Reformation English Catholicism, in practice, as a continuation of medieval Christianity; on the other hand we cannot regard it as something totally different." More directly on the Marian field, Edward Norman (The English Catholic Church in the Nineteenth Century. Oxford, Clarendon Press, 1984) commenting on the rivalry between the Ultramontanist/neo-classical Italianate structures and Traditional English/Gothic structures, notes a difference in styles of worship between the two. "Yet in all truth, the traditional worship of the "old Catholics" with its rejection of continental devotional practices - a rejection which extended to images of the Virgin, votive candles, processions, and so forth - was, like Anglican worship at the start of the 19th century, extremely plain and subdued in tone." Perhaps he fails to note that English Catholics may have become accustomed to this restraint simply from the necessity of avoiding drawing dangerous attention. In the minds of more than one group, some within the Anglican tradition, some in communion with Rome by upbringing or by reconciliation due to their experience of the Oxford Movement, a sense of recovery of the medieval status and institutions of the Catholic tradition motivated an effort that was from a similar starting point and, because separated, inevitably directed at a goal that would either need to be shared or ultimately would cause great conflict. Regrettably, for a substantial period of the century of restoration, it was the latter that hallmarked the efforts of Christians at Walsingham.

With the above serving as a setting or background, we are at the penultimate stage before revival of the public cult and being very close now to the brief of other contributors to the Conference, I must not encroach on what they will be dealing with. What I must say is that at this point a range of powerful personalities was to emerge on the Walsingham stage and a complexity of different stances was to ultimately confuse people who shared the same objective of revival of the cult of Our Lady of Walsingham. Within the Oxford Movement had been a conviction that restoration of religious life would contribute to the revival of the Catholic faith. Among those committed to this view was Miss Charlotte Pearson Boyd (1837-1906), who was to work unstintingly for re-union between the Anglican communion and Rome and also to promote Benedictine life both as an Anglican and subsequently as a Roman Catholic. She included in her circle of friends and associates, Dom Bede Camm, Dom Philibert Feasey and Hugh Edmund Ford, the Prior of Downside, Dom Aidan Gasquet et al. Her involvement with and efforts over the Slipper Chapel, which she thought of as Benedictine land through its link with the medieval cell at Horsham St. Faith, were to bring disappointment and pain in her dealing with Bishop Arthur Riddell of Northampton, though her efforts were to have such a long term importance for Walsingham. From that same Oxford Movement emerged Fr. Philip Fletcher (1848-1928) as a gifted High Churchman who spent the last phase of his Anglican life as curate at St. Bartholomew's, Brighton, before being reconciled to Rome in 1882. Two years later in 1884, the Rev. Arthur D. Wagner established a Walsingham chapel at St. Mary's, Buxted, to which latter the Rev. Colin Stephenson referred as "Fr. Wagner's country paradise for Anglo-Catholics". This act was to have long term influence also. As Master of the Guild of Our Lady of Ransom, which he had launched, Fletcher in co-operation with Fr. Wrigglesworth of King's Lynn, secured the establishment of the revived cult of Our Lady of Walsingham in the parish of his friend. Though not sharing precisely equivalent dates, a true son of the Tractarian Movement was an interesting parallel to Fletcher, Fr. Alfred Hope Patten (1885-1958) spent time at Buxted as a curate later and, while there, is said to have read all that he could to learn about the pre-Reformation shrine. The outcome for the three was markedly different. Prior to 1897, Boyd and Fletcher were led to make a decision of change to be reconciled to Rome. This was to shape their behaviour in regard to Walsingham. They had to work with the understanding of jurisdiction and ecclesiastical authority that went with the territory. There was no scope for idiosyncratic or individualistic decisions as long as the Bishop had to be considered. Hope Patten went along with that vision of the Western Church, holding the ecclesiastical position of 'Papalist' within the Anglican Church which involves complete obedience to the Holy See in all things but reserves private judgement re. Anglican Orders and he also subscribed to a notion of dispersed authority which enabled action at variance with the mind of his bishop. In the case of all three, we can see how past remembrance and hope for revival went as so often is the case in wildly different direction from those desired. Had Walsingham been an encounter of completely opposite views of Mary, then the ground might have been clearer. Due to the way non-conformism at Walsingham experienced a debilitating decline for complex reasons, there was no notable resistance to the reintroduction into the village of things Marian from that quarter. It seems the issue was never, therefore, that of opposing views on Mary herself but one of differing ecclesiologies, and at times all the harder because of that.

The past then is our present thinking about what went on before us. We cannot falsify the thinking of the participants in the past, but we can see it in a new light. To avoid a repetition of the worst outcomes of history, we need to remain steadfast in addressing real difficulties by an ecumenism of the head in harmony with an ecumenism of the heart. On the principle of doing together what we are able to do, Walsingham's devotion to Our Lady seeks to express a pilgrim way forward with honesty and mutual respect, building certainly on the strength of the past while moving away from those divisive experiences that are also part of the intervening past that lay between the glorious days of the medieval shrine and what came to be restored.

THE CHARLOTTE BOYD CONNECTION

by Ethel Hostler

I'd like to begin by thanking all those concerned for inviting me to give one of the talks at this Centenary Conference. My sole qualification for standing before you today is a passionate interest in my subject matter. (Indeed, a friend of mine has called my interest in Miss Charlotte Pearson Boyd "a pathological obsession"!) I trust it is not quite that, but I do hope to share with you this morning something of the affection and admiration that I feel for this remarkable lady, without whose faith, foresight and great generosity we would not be celebrating this centenary at all.

To tell the story of Miss Boyd we must travel back many years in time, and across many miles of land and sea. Back to the early 19th century, and to the Far East, to China, where in March 1837 the following announcement appeared in the *Canton Register:*

BIRTH
At Macao, on the 21st instant
the Lady of A. P. Boyd, Esq.
of a daughter.

Thus is recorded the birth of one among the lesser known but most deserving of remembrance of the daughters of the Church. She was the firstborn of Alexander Pearson Boyd, a merchant based at Canton, and his wife Charlotte (née Buckle) - she was born a Benedictine (on 21st March, Feast of St. Benedict) and the name of her birthplace, 'Macao', means 'City of God'. What could be more appropriate?

Miss Boyd's ancestry was distinguished on both sides. One William Boyd was in 1451 Abbot of Kilwinning[1], a rich and famous Benedictine monastery in Ayrshire; the Boyd family seat was Dean Castle, a few miles away at Kilmarnock. Another William Boyd, the fourth Earl of Kilmarnock, chose the wrong side in the 1745 Rebellion, was captured at the Battle of Culloden and later executed on Tower Hill. A touring exhibition about Bonnie Prince Charlie came to London a year or so ago, and on display there was the very basket-hilted broadsword that Earl William was wielding at Culloden, its hilt inscribed with his initials "W.E.K.". On the wall behind it was a graphic

Charlotte Boyd

print of the executions on Tower Hill of the Jacobite Earls of Kilmarnock and of Cromartie, and Lords Balmerino and Lovat. In the corners of this print were cameos of these four unfortunates, and I found myself looking at the Boyd family face - that square, rather heavy jawline, but with a sweetly modelled mouth - as may be seen in the only known portrait of Miss Boyd herself, which hangs in the Slipper Chapel.

As for the Buckles, Charlotte's mother's side of the family, Sir Cuthbert Buckle, a vintner from Westmoreland, settled in London, where he prospered. He was twice Master of the Vintners' Company, and Lord Mayor of London in 1593. He owned 33 Mark Lane, in the City, a fine old house later to be the headquarters of the firm of Buckle, Boyd and Buckle, ship owners, marine and insurance brokers and wine merchants. Charlotte's grandfather, John William Buckle, by marrying as his first wife a Miss Sarah Boyd, had united two families of thriving businessmen. Charlotte's merchant uncle William Smith Boyd had his business premises in Moorgate Street, London, and owned estates and plantations on the Malabar coast of India. So, although, alas, there appears to be little record of Miss Boyd's childhood years, we know that she did grow up in prosperous circumstances, though not in China. She was baptised there, in the British Chapel at Macao, on 27th April 1837, by the Chaplain to the East India Company, the Rev. George Harvey Vachell, but the Boyd family set sail for London only six weeks after Charlotte's birth. Why did they embark on such a long and hazardous voyage so soon, with a convalescent mother and a tiny baby? Possibly because staying in China at that time might well have been an even greater hazard. There was long-standing friction between European traders and the Chinese authorities, and although warfare did not break out until the first of the so-called 'Opium Wars' in 1839, the situation was pretty dangerous.

So the Boyd family returned to England, where it grew in number. Charlotte was the first of five children. A brother, Pearson, was born in 1838 at Turville Park, Buckinghamshire, and a second brother, John William, in 1840 at Pinkney House, Pinkneys Green, Berkshire. Each boy in turn was brought to the City of London to be baptised at St. Olave's, Hart Street, where their parents had been married. By 1845 the Boyds were living in Brighton, at 24 Lewes Crescent, Kemp Town, where a sister, Eliza Isabella, was born that year, to be followed by the youngest of the family, Sarah Emily, who was born in 1846. Lewes Crescent was a prestigious address - the 6th Duke of Devonshire, owner of Chatsworth and other stately piles, had bought 1 Lewes Crescent as his 'marine residence'.

We come now to a very significant date and place in Charlotte's life - the date 1850, the place Glastonbury Abbey. Miss Boyd herself recorded this event twenty-eight years later in *Our Work,* a journal produced by the Sisters of the Church[2], an Anglican Community based then in Kilburn in north-west London. Recalling a visit to Glastonbury Abbey as a member of a pleasure-party, Miss Boyd wrote that she

> ... a young girl at the time, sat alone on that summer afternoon, sadly contemplating the ruins in their desolation and desecration. Impelled by a sudden impulse, she knelt and offered herself to the work of restoration, if God would accept her. Quickly and silently the years passed by, while the desire then kindled in her heart was meantime mentioned only to God in prayer, till in 1865, when Dr Neale[3] was sought as a counsellor, his words, "I would have you take this as your work in life," encouraged and confirmed the purpose formed so long before. It was not, however, until 1875 that a practical beginning could be made; the Fathers of Cowley[4] kindly giving the scheme their countenance and support, and undertaking the responsibility of administering the Trust in its present form...

Thus with the investment by Miss Boyd of £500 in Russian Bonds was founded the English Abbey Restoration Trust,[5] with three members of the Society of St. John the Evangelist as the first Trustees. This venture was well supported - within three years it had almost 1,000 members, including 13 Religious Communities and 440 Priests. The object of the Trust was to provide funds for the purchase of ancient ecclesiastical buildings which had passed into secular hands, and their restoration for worship according to the rites of the Church of England.

During the 1860s death took its toll of Charlotte's immediate family: her sister Eliza Isabella died of tuberculosis aged 15; her brother Pearson, a Lieutenant in the Bengal Infantry, died in India aged 25; her youngest sister Sarah Emily died aged 22; her father died in 1864, her mother in 1867. Charlotte's surviving sibling, John William, had taken Holy Orders and from 1864-66 was serving his first curacy at St. Barnabas, Addison Road, Kensington, while living nearby with his parents at 6 Argyll Road.

Whilst awaiting the opportunity for her English Abbey Restoration Trust to purchase its first building, Charlotte herself had begun her philanthropic work in a most practical way, by founding in 1865 the Orphanage of the Infant Saviour. Originally at Lansdowne Terrace, Kensington, this orphanage was moved to Kilburn in 1871, where it grew and flourished. The census return for 1871 listed 27 girls; that of 1881 55; and by 1891 there were 107 orphans, including two little boys, Robert Atkins aged 2 and Edward P. Morris aged 1. Miss Boyd remained living simply as the resident head of her Orphanage from its inception until her death forty years later.

It was not only orphaned children who benefited from Miss Boyd's care; in the Annual Report for 1902 she records that

> ... six gentlewomen have received hospitality in time of distress, and remained with us until suitable employment was found for them. Servants out of work or in bad health have been taken into the Home for rest and care. Children have been temporarily sheltered while their mothers were in various hospitals...

In 1871, the year that Miss Boyd moved her Orphanage from Kensington to Kilburn, the Rev. Richard Carr Kirkpatrick became the founder Vicar of St. Augustine's, Kilburn, which over the next ten years evolved into a large and beautiful building wherein worship took a firm Anglo-Catholic form. It is recorded that Father Kirkpatrick was in love with Miss Boyd when they were both young, but that "he found his hopes doomed to disappointment."

Unlike many a Victorian lady, Miss Boyd could afford not to marry, and she chose to remain independent. By 1881 she had her own Orphanage Chapel, built in the Gothic style and furnished in the High Church tradition, including an altar cross formed from the jewelled processional cross that she had commissioned to be presented to the first Abbey to be restored by her English Abbey Restoration Trust. Among Miss Boyd's honorary chaplains were Reginald Camm and Henry Worth, then fellow curates at St. Agnes, Kennington Park.

Our story moves now into the Kentish countryside. Nineteenth century London was an unhealthy place for young children, and when in 1883 Mrs Isabella Akers, owner of Malling Abbey, formerly an 11th century Benedictine foundation, offered its 14th century Gatehouse and Pilgrim Chapel to the English Abbey Restoration Trust, Miss Boyd made use of the buildings as a country retreat for her Kilburn orphans. Miss Boyd had known West Malling for some ten years; she recalled that on her first visit she had gone down to Gundulf's St. Leonard's Tower and drunk a cup of water from the so-called 'wishing well'. Her wish was that she might buy Gundulf's Abbey some day - as indeed she did, though not until almost 20 years later.

Come with me now to rural Middlesex, to Feltham, where in 1868 that extraordinary eccentric Father Ignatius[7] whose life-story you can read in Arthur Calder-Marshall's entertaining book *The Enthusiast,* had founded an Anglican Benedictine Sisterhood called the Congregation of St. Mary and St. Scholastica. In 1883 a London clergyman who had this small community's interests at heart, took Miss Boyd to meet the nuns. He had told their Reverend Mother Hilda Stewart that Miss Boyd "was very rich and might do great things for the Community" - as indeed she later did, but it does not seem to have been love at first sight on either side! One of the nuns, Dame Paulina Bridges, wrote in her '*Memories*' of autumn 1883:

> A clergyman brought a lady down to see Rev. Mother. A certain Miss Boyd. She evidently did not like us at the time, and she did not come again. The next year she came down again by herself and stayed a few days. Rev. Mother did not seem to take to her very much, and we thought no more about her. During the Octave of the Assumption in 1886 she asked to become an Associate Sister, taking the name of Sr. Scholastica. When the nuns asked Rev. Mother at recreation what she thought of her, she said: "I don't think she will

> come much, or be of much use to us. She has not grasped any ideas of the Benedictine life. It was only seeing the other associates caught her fancy. Well, we shall see."

What **we** see is how wrong Mother Hilda was! Her small Community lived in great poverty and had few benefactors, but among the most generous and faithful was Miss Boyd. She continued to support the nuns when in 1889 they had to move from Feltham to Twickenham, acquiring a house near their Priory, which she ran as an Orphanage for boys, and when in 1893 the Community had to move yet again, Miss Boyd offered them Malling Abbey, which she had bought the previous year for £10,000.

Miss Boyd had not been the only person desirous of acquiring Malling Abbey. In her 'Memories' of 1892, Dame Paulina records that:

> Miss Boyd was having trouble with lawyers. There were some Americans in London, offering a high price for the Abbey, they wish to make it and the grounds into tea gardens! One man was actually in the office when she went to sign the Deed. But she got the Abbey!

One of the things I was asked to try to find out was where Miss Boyd got her money from. She inherited her fortune not from her father, who at his death in 1864 had left under £600, but from other members of the Buckle and Boyd families, and principally from her uncle Judge John Buckle. On his death in 1891 he bequeathed

> to my niece Charlotte Pearson Boyd the picture of her mother, Murillo's picture of the Virgin and that of the Holy Sepulchre, also my crimson silk quilt and eiderdown quilt... and all my property except the special bequests to others.

As these special bequests were relatively minor, Miss Boyd inherited the bulk of her uncle's personal estate, valued at £19,226.16.2. And I was so relieved to find this - I had been dreading the possibility of having to tell the nuns that Malling Abbey had been bought with the proceeds of the illegal opium trade in China! But it was almost certainly with £10,000 of Judge John's bequest that Miss Boyd made her historic purchase in 1892.

At this point in Miss Boyd's life, Rome loomed on the horizon. In 1890 Reginald Camm, one of her High Anglican priest friends, converted to Rome, and entered Maredsous Abbey in Belgium, taking at his clothing as a Benedictine Novice the name of Bede. Miss Boyd was fond of this young man and she went to Maredsous to visit him on several occasions, once after attending a performance of the Passion Play at Oberammagau, and in 1893 she expressed a wish to found at Maredsous a daily Mass, to be said "for the union of the Churches". This wording did not meet with official approval, so Miss Boyd proposed instead that the Mass should be offered "that England, in the matter of religion, should do the will of God." This was accepted, and she returned to England to seek out in prayer what should be the will of God for **her.**

Mother Hilda and her nuns moved to Malling Abbey on Easter Tuesday 1893. Their journey was not straightforward. Some of the nuns went by train, but most travelled in a procession of horse-drawn carts. It is a long way from Twickenham to West Malling by horse and cart, even longer when your leading driver misses a turning and takes you round in a circle! Dame Paulina described their arrival:

> Miss Boyd had got very anxious, as those who went by train had arrived sooner, and were quite sure some accident had happened. It had got so dark, she sent to the village and hired some lamps and put them in windows facing the road over the fields. Also she lit up the little gatehouse chapel. She had a lot of candles ready as she had arranged with Rev. Mother and the Chaplain to get down just inside the arch of the gatehouse and go up to the Abbey in procession, singing the 68th psalm. The Chaplain had brought the processional cross and censer, so in a few minutes we were ready, and the procession moved up the drive, through the garth and cloisters to the room which Miss Boyd had got ready for a Chapel. We then sang the Te Deum and Compline.

So, after 355 years, Benedictines were once again giving glory to God at Malling Abbey. Miss Boyd's girlhood aspiration had been realised.

It is related that as soon as the Community had settled in the Abbey they were conscious of the pre-Reformation nuns in their midst. Miss Boyd herself, while staying at the Abbey, maintained that on two successive nights she had

Slipper Chapel 1891.

been visited by them, and that they had urged her to take some important step. They were not specific as to what that step should be, but later, when Miss Boyd was received into the Roman Catholic Church, she was convinced that this was what her nocturnal visitors had wanted. Meantime Miss Boyd persevered in "building up the waste places", and we follow her now northwards, into East Anglia to Walsingham, where, after an unsuccessful attempt in 1893 to purchase the Priory from its owner, Henry Lee Warner, she began negotiations to buy from him the Slipper Chapel[8] just outside Walsingham itself. By the time Miss Boyd saw it, this tiny chapel was in a sadly ruinous state, having been used over the years as a cowshed, as a barn, and as tenement dwellings, but she had great hopes and plans for it.

Negotiations for its purchase took two years, and during this time Miss Boyd's own life had taken a critical turn. This event, which took place at the close of a further visit to Fr. Bede Camm at Maredsous, is recorded in the *Annals of the English Convent* at Bruges, from which I quote:

> On September 16th 1894, Fr. Clarke S.J. gave our retreat. At the close of it, he gained to the Church a valuable soul, Miss Boyd, a ritualist, who had long been wavering and on whom many other souls depended. She had an orphanage in London, and was surrounded by Anglican ministers who kept her from following her convictions. But the Community prayed earnestly for her in the retreat. Fr. Clarke was a man of prayer and had the grace to remove

all her doubts; she was received into the Church on the 22nd. She made her First Communion on the 23rd.

Miss Boyd left England an Anglican, she returned a Roman Catholic, and found herself faced with enormous problems. Quite apart from the breach with many of her long-standing close friends, she, a Catholic, owned a large Orphanage and School with Anglican orphans, staff and trustees. Thomas Fish Marson, Miss Boyd's solicitor cousin and a trustee of her Kilburn Orphanage, disapproved so strongly of her proposal to turn it into a Roman Catholic institution and hand it over to Downside Abbey that he went to the Charities Commission in an attempt to prevent this. The local Roman Catholics do not seem to have given their new convert a very warm welcome. They were suspicious and disapproving when she did not instantly dismiss all the Anglicans in her charge and replace them with Catholics. This was not Miss Boyd's way; she showed more love and compassion to those in her care, allowing her Orphanage and School to become Catholic through natural wastage. This process took four years, and it was not until the end of 1898 that her Orphanage Chapel was licensed for Catholic Mass.

Having completed the purchase of the Slipper Chapel in 1896, Miss Boyd applied to the English Abbey Restoration Trust for a grant towards its restoration, but the Trustees were obliged to refuse, as she herself had

Workmen at work on the Slipper Chapel.

specified that Trust funds were to be used only for buildings where worship followed the rites of the Church of England. So, at her own expense, Miss Boyd employed the architect Thomas Garner[9] to restore the Slipper Chapel and build a priest's house next to it, and she gifted it to Downside Abbey. This unfortunately led to problems and difficulties in the long term. Writing to her friend the author Dudley Baxter in 1903, Miss Boyd said:

> There is an endowment on the Slipper Chapel, and we had hoped ere this Holy Mass would have been said daily for the conversion of England, and souls would have been gathered in.

So what was the problem? The Chapel had been restored some six years previously, why still no Mass there? Well, it seems to have been a Bishop - Bishop Arthur Riddell of Northampton - who was the stumbling-block. In a further letter to Dudley Baxter Miss Boyd states frankly:

> The Bishop, I feel, will be our great obstacle in the matter of Walsingham. His known dislike of the regulars - especially Benedictines - has prevented a mission at Walsingham for years.

This is a sad and regrettable episode. In 1895 Miss Boyd had written to the Bishop concerning the Slipper Chapel:

> It is old Benedictine ground and I had a great wish to restore it to them... Would your Lordship accept the Benedictines should it be possible for them to take a Mission near Walsingham? Or have you any suggestion to make regarding the Chapel.

In reply, thanking Miss Boyd for the good work of restoring so celebrated a spot as the Slipper Chapel of Walsingham, the Bishop wrote:

> ...for years I have longed to do something for the North district of Norfolk and I begin to see in your work the realisation of my hopes. In answer to your questions I may say that I should like to place a good missionary priest at the Slipper Chapel...

Two years later in 1897 Miss Boyd wrote again to Bishop Riddell:

> Thinking you will be interested I am sending you a lithograph of the Slipper Chapel at Walsingham as it is to be. At present only a plain

> stone Altar and the Shrine of our Ladye of Walsingham is promised .....The property is invested in the names of three of the Downside Benedictine Fathers, ...

Miss Boyd concluded:

> It is hoped in time to endow a Mass there for the conversion of England and to form it with your kind permission into a Mission Station. But this is in the far distance and the Chapel can only be a place of pilgrimage at present.

The Bishop, alas, remained implacably opposed to Miss Boyd's hopes, and only one religious function took place in the Slipper Chapel during her lifetime. On 19th August 1897, the shrine at Kings Lynn was opened: on 20th August there was a pilgrimage from Kings Lynn to the Slipper Chapel. Among those who signed the list of pilgrims was Mary B. Boyd of Kilburn. (Mary being the name she took at her reception into the Roman Catholic Church, B standing for Benedict, marking her oblation.)

Writing again to Dudley Baxter in 1904 about their hopes that a continental community acceptable to the Bishop might settle at Walsingham, Miss Boyd said:

> it will be better to ask the Rev. Mother to communicate with you direct, knowing how unsavoury I am in the Bishop's nostrils - it will be well for me to keep as the 'power behind the Pope'. If this plan is carried out I will undertake the 1st quarter's house rent.

This plan, it appears, was not carried out. A letter from The Orphanage, Percy Road, dated 30th September 1904 reads:

> Dear Mr. Baxter,
> I am answering your letter for Miss Boyd, as her eyes are very bad just now. Respecting poor Walsingham, Miss Boyd says the Abbot has asked for permission to open the Slipper Chapel and have Mass said there and been refused. He does not wish to write again, as the Bishop did not answer his last letter. Miss Boyd says that as soon as she sees the least sign of relaxation on the part of the Bishop she will let you know. She has been advised to write to Rome about the matter but must wait patiently. W.M.B.

Miss Boyd did indeed show great faith and patience during the last ten years of her life, when, despite her disappointment at the Bishop's repeated refusal to allow any services in the Slipper Chapel, she steadfastly believed that

> ... the shrine will be restored and we have only need of a little more prayer and patience and Walsingham will have a Catholic centre and Holy Mass will be restored.

Alas, it took more than "a little more prayer and patience" - not until 1934 was Mass once again celebrated in the Slipper Chapel at Walsingham.

We must now make a brief excursion to a leafy suburb of West London. Prior Edmund Ford, later to be the first Abbot of Downside, had become Miss Boyd's trusted friend and adviser, and when in 1896 Downside established a Mission at Ealing, Miss Boyd, generous as ever, gave help and support to this venture. By 1903 she had leased 56 Windsor Road, Ealing, and established there a small orphanage, with one room fitted up as a Chapel-of-ease, but the local Catholic congregation soon outgrew this provision. In 1904 Miss Boyd wrote:

> Our present house is quite unsuited to the growing needs of the Mission (worshippers now sit on our stairs!)

In October of that year she told Abbot Ford that she had completed the purchase of Glastonbury House, Grange Road, Ealing, and had had it put in the names of the trustees of the Ealing Mission. A map of 19th century Ealing shows Glastonbury House as a large property with an extensive garden. Miss Boyd proposed to establish there an Orphanage dedicated to Our Lady of Walsingham, together with a more spacious Chapel-of-ease. The very name of the house must have had an instant appeal for Miss Boyd, recalling as it did that first visit to Glastonbury 54 years previously, when as a young girl she had vowed to build up the waste places and give them back to God.

Writing to Prior Ford in 1895 that she hoped to join the pilgrimage to Glastonbury Tor, she had said:

> Blessed Richard Whiting[10] was the hero of my youth, and my whole life took on fresh colouring at the old Abbey.

Miss Boyd's life on earth though was drawing to its close. For some years she had suffered from diabetes, and complications had begun to set in. Her letter to Abbot Ford dated 23rd May 1904 concludes:

> I trust that you are well and flourishing? For myself I am drifting into darkness - my eyes having failed me.

Miss Boyd lived on, a semi-invalid but continuing to take a keen interest in religious affairs, until 3rd April 1906, when at 7.00 p.m. she died at her Orphanage in Kilburn. She was buried in Holy Week in St. Mary's Roman Catholic cemetery, Kensal Green in grave No. 3038. Sadly for many years her grave remained without any memorial, until in the 1960s Martin Gillett, an admirer and champion of Miss Boyd, went to considerable trouble to remedy this. He persuaded the Abbot of Downside to give for Miss Boyd's grave an iron cross such as she would have had, had she, as a Benedictine oblate, been buried in the graveyard there, and on the anniversary of her death, 3rd April 1962, a touching ceremony took place at Kensal Green cemetery. In Martin Gillett's words:

> At last Miss Boyd has her memorial and that given by the Abbot President, and put up by a Cardinal Archbishop, and blessed by the Cardinal's delegate in the presence of the representative of the Lord Bishop of Northampton, ...

(Sadly, yet another Bishop of Northampton appears to have looked unfavourably on Miss Boyd. Martin Gillett had hoped Bishop Parker would have blessed her memorial, but the Bishop asked Fr. Gerard Hulme, priest in charge of the Shrine at Walsingham, to represent him, writing that he "disliked going to London just for this.")

Charlotte Boyd's renovated grave, St. Mary's Cemetery, Kensal Green.

In 1980, because of proposed alterations at the Kensal Green cemetery, Miss Boyd's cross, together with the inscribed headstone, was moved to Walsingham, and placed on the outside wall of the Slipper Chapel. A simple stone plaque was put in its place on the bedstone at Kensal, and recently the stonework and lettering have been beautifully cleaned and restored by an anonymous benefactor.

What remains of Miss Boyd's endeavours today? Outwardly, two buildings: Malling Abbey, still inhabited by Anglican Benedictines (though not the descendants of Miss Boyd's original nuns - they became Roman Catholics in 1913, by which time they had moved to St. Bride's, Milford Haven) and the Slipper Chapel, Walsingham, now the world-famous English National Shrine of Our Lady, whose centenary we celebrate this year, Miss Boyd, I am sure, rejoicing with us. Miss Boyd's various orphanages were phased out long ago, but there must still be living those who are descended from the many orphans cared for during the 40 and more years her institutions were in being.

Miss Boyd's quiet influence on her contemporaries must have been considerable. Her many friends ranged from Lord Halifax's late Chaplain to an engine driver in Kent, who, she wrote:

> ... has taken to the penny Catechism and attending a Catholic church - he comes up from Deal to spend Sunday with me.

In a letter to Abbot Ford in 1903, Miss Boyd wrote:

> I have made a very interesting friend lately - Lord Halifax's late Chaplain... he thinks the world is too strong for Lord H's conversion (he is made so much of in Rome by the Cardinal as an English nobleman) but we know how light penetrates the darkness.

A number of people associated with Miss Boyd did indeed follow her on the road to Rome - among these were her priest friends Henry Worth and Henry Feasey (who became Dom Philibert Feasey OSB of Ramsgate Abbey); Thomas Garner (the architect she employed to restore the Slipper Chapel); both the Malling Abbey Chaplains; and the Archbishop of Canterbury's son, the Rev. Robert Hugh Benson.[11] Miss Boyd herself had kept open house for ex-Anglican Sisters who were finding their way to Rome. As Henry Worth wrote of her to the Abbess of Stanbrook:

> They all found in her a haven of refuge; no-one who turned to her was ever refused.

This statement doubtless helps to explain what happened to Miss Boyd's fortune. So great had been her generosity that by as early as 1895 she was obliged, in reply to an appeal for financial help from Fr. Ethelbert Taunton, to write:

> I too am in Queer Street as regards my yearly income. Xmas brings me liabilities up to over £130 and all I know of to meet it is about £110 - but I should like to help you and if the Prior consents to letting you have £50 out of what is in his hands for the Slipper Chapel I will gladly endorse it...I fear these are hard times for everyone. I had two sad appeals from old friends yesterday - one who has decided to go to the Workhouse as soon as Xmas is past, poor thing.

By 1903 Miss Boyd had very little ready money left. Writing to Dudley Baxter of their 'shared desire to restore devotion to Our Lady at Walsingham', she said:

> I was once rich, but founding Masses and buying Malling Abbey and the Slipper Chapel, with the support of my two orphanages and over 80 children has not left me much now at my command.

When Miss Boyd died in 1906 Abbot Ford wrote a memorandum listing her gifts to Downside as:

1. Slipper Chapel
2. Kilburn Orphanage
3. Glastonbury House, Ealing
4. £2,000 Brazilian bonds (at Downside)
5. £1,200 (?) [in trust with Harratt - solicitor]

Miss Boyd's Will, made on 1st December 1898, left her estate and effects 'to the Prior of Downside for the time being at my death'. When her Will was proved, on 7th July 1906, her effects were valued at £3,389 12. 4d. Such were Miss Boyd's material bequests; her spiritual ones were far greater.

The Boyds were proud of their descent from the Scottish Earls of Kilmarnock[12]. When Charlotte's wealthy merchant uncle William Smith Boyd purchased in Kensal Green cemetery a large vault wherein and whereon 22 members of her family are interred or commemorated, he had emblazoned on the obelisk the Boyd family crest, a right hand raised in benediction, with the motto '*Confido', ('I trust').* Finding this monument was one of the highlights of my quest, but as I stood knee-deep among the nettles reading the inscriptions I noticed one intriguing omission. The name of Charlotte's brother the Rev. John William Boyd is there, as are those of the two of his ten children who pre-deceased him, William Marson Stuart Boyd aged 8, and Evelyn Mary Boyd, aged 3. Between his name and theirs is a space - a wife-shaped space - but Mrs Edith Louisa Leath Boyd is not there. After bringing up her surviving eight children she moved to Reigate in Surrey, where she bought a large house called 'The Laurels' which she re-named 'Kilmarnock'. She spent the last years of her life at the Mostyn Private Hotel, Eastbourne, where she died aged 78 in 1923 leaving the sum of £31,119 9s. 11d and a request in her Will that 'a suitable memorial be erected to my memory'. That suitable memorial I have as yet not found.

So although my three year search has yielded a Family Tree of 144 names, there are still some unattached twiglets, and although there was more than enough material for a 20-page booklet, the work is still entitled *Some notes on the life of Charlotte Boyd.* It is possible that more information about this somewhat elusive lady and her extended family may yet come to light, aand if any of you who have listened so patiently to my attempt to keep her memory green do come across further facts, I would be delighted to hear of them.

REFERENCES

1. **Kilwinning** takes its name from St. Winnin, or Wynin, an Irish saint who flourished in the 8th century, and whose fame led to the foundation in 1140 of a rich and celebrated Benedictine Abbey by Hugh de Morville, Lord of Cunningham and High Constable of Scotland in the reign of David I. The Abbey was largely destroyed in the 16th century, and only a small part of the ruins remain.
2. **Sisters of the Church.** An Anglican community founded in 1870 by Miss Emily Ayckbourn to care for and educate orphans and the children of the poor. The Mother House and Orphanage of Mercy at Kilburn in north-west London was bombed in the Second World War and the community is now at Ham Common, Surrey.
3. **The Rev. John Mason Neale** (1818-66). A persecuted ritualist, Warden from 1846 of Sackville College almshouse, and founder of the Anglican Society of St. Margaret at East Grinstead in 1855. Translator of many hymns from the Latin and Greek, including "All glory, laud and honour"; "The day of Resurrection" and "Christ is made the sure Foundation".
4. **The Fathers of Cowley**. In 1866 Richard Meux Benson founded the Society of St. John the Evangelist, the first stable religious community for men in the Church of England since the Reformation. The Rule he drew up was for the 'Mixed Life', one in which the practice of contemplation is mingled with exterior activities. The priests and

brothers came to be called 'Cowley Fathers' after the location of their Mother House in Oxford.

5. **The English Abbey Restoration Trust.** Two *Occasional Papers* survive: - extracts - Number 1: February 1887. The history of the English Abbey Restoration Trust during the last 10 years has been rather that of waiting than doing active work. In 1883 the Gate House of Malling Abbey was placed at the disposal of the promoters of the Trust through the generous kindness of its owner. It has been utilized as a small orphanage, and has attached to it a beautifully restored Chapel, to which the Vicar of the Parish is glad to welcome any Clergy who wish to assist in its services. Rev. D. J. Mackey, Cleeton St. Mary Vicarage, Cleeton Mortimer, Salop.

Number 2: November 1892. This Trust has now after nearly thirty years of waiting entered upon a new stage - one of activity.

The Benedictine Abbey of Malling in Kent, founded in the 11th century by Gundulf, Bishop of Rochester, has at length after three and a half centuries been restored to the Church. A Sisterhood observing the ancient Rule hope to take possession in the Spring, when once again the Divine Office so long silenced will be recited day by day, and the One Sacrifice be daily pleaded.

This would seem to be the crown of the work begun by the late possessors of the Abbey, who, having restored the Gate House Chapel, devoted the Gate House itself to the purposes of a work of charity. (Unsigned, but thought to have been written by Miss Boyd herself.)

6. **Gundulf.** In 1090 Gundulf, monk of Bec and Bishop of Rochester, founded Malling Abbey for Benedictine nuns. He also built nearby one of the first great Norman keeps, the building known today as St. Leonard's Tower. In the 14th century this was used as a cell of Malling Abbey, where a small group of nuns could live together.

7. **Father Ignatius.** Joseph Leycester Lyne was the first and one of the most eccentric and bizarre figures in the story of the revival of the religious life in the Church of England. In 1863 he founded a monastery at Claydon, Suffolk, later moving the brothers to Norwich, then to Laleham in Middlesex and finally to Llanthony in Wales. From 1868, when he installed Emily Stewart as Mother Hilda, Prioress of the Benedictine Community he founded at Feltham in Middlesex, he attempted to impose his wilful and autocratic rule on the nuns, until in 1878 they rebelled, and insisted on directing their own affairs, with Mother Hilda recognised as Abbess.

8. **The Slipper Chapel** was built at Houghton, about a mile and a half outside Little Walsingham itself. According to popular tradition, it was at this tiny 14th century chapel that pilgrims removed their shoes, to finish their pilgrimage to the Holy House at Walsingham Priory barefoot.

9. **Thomas Garner** (1839-1906) A pupil of Sir George Gilbert Scott, he worked in partnership with George Frederick Bodley from 1869-97. His largest solo commission was to build in 1901-05 in the neo-Gothic style the choir and sanctuary of the Basilica of St. Gregory the Great, Downside Abbey Church, where he himself lies buried.

10. **Blessed Richard Whiting**. The last Abbot of Glastonbury, he was hanged. drawn and quartered on Glastonbury Tor on 15th November 1539.

11. **Robert Hugh Benson** while a curate at Kemsing in Kent, often went over to Malling Abbey, and his impressions of it are recorded in the story 'In the Convent Chapel' in his book *The Light Invisible,* published in 1903. Writing in the person of the old priest, Benson describes how a lay sister invited him into the parlour, from where he could see out into the

garden and across to the grave-yard. Then the Reverend Mother, 'a wonderful, dignified little old lady with a quiet wrinkled face' came in, and after some minutes of conversation took him across the garth to the chapel in the old south transept. After the bright sunlight it seemed very dark, and only gradually did he become aware of the figure of a nun kneeling in prayer before the blessed Sacrament. From thoughts of pity and even of irritation at the uselessness of her life, he suddenly became aware that the atmosphere was charged with energy; great powers seemed to be astir, and this black figure knelt at the centre of reality and force as the currents of need and grace went to and fro. "From this peaceful chapel radiated lines of spiritual power, bewildering in their profusion and terrible in the intensity of their hidden fire."
12. **The Boyds of Kilmarnock**. "... the ruins of Dean Castle, once the seat of the noble, but unfortunate family of Boyd, are situated within a mile and a half of Kilmarnock. They stand on a gentle rising ground on the banks of the Kilmarnock, formerly called, according to tradition, the Carth water:-

> The Water of Carth rins by the Dean,
> That ance was Lord Boyd's lodgin',
> The Lord wi' the loupen han',
> He lost his title and his lan'.

This rhyme refers to the last Earl of Kilmarnock, who forfeited his title and estates by taking part in the rebellion of 1745. The 'loupen hand' is an allusion to the crest of the family, which is a dexter hand, couped at the wrist, erect, pointing with the thumb and the two next fingers, the others turning down, with the motto, 'Confido'." [from A *History of the Counties of Ayr and Wigan* Vol. III, by James Paterson, Edinburgh, 1866.)

SOURCES CONSULTED

Archives of the R.C. National Shrine, Walsingham
Archives of the R.C. Diocese of East Anglia, Norwich
Downside Abbey archives
Malling Abbey archives
Kent County archives, Maidstone
Office of Population Censuses and Surveys, St. Catherine's House
Public Records Office (Chancery Lane, Kew)
Somerset House - Wills
Guildhall Library & Manuscript Library
Greater London Record Office & History Library
India Office (British Library)
British Museum Newspaper Library
National Register of Archives
Lambeth Palace Library
Catholic Central Library
Henry Worth correspondence, Stanbrook Abbey
Kensington local studies collection

Kilburn local history collection, Cricklewood Library
Archives of St. Augustine's Church, Kilburn
English Abbey Restoration Trust archives, St. Edward's House, Westminster
Local history collection, Hither Green Library
Borough of Lambeth archives, Minet Library
Southwark local studies library
Local history collection, Harrow Library
Ealing local history library
Camden local studies collection
Maritime Information Centre, Greenwich
County Record Office, Berkshire
County Record Office, Buckinghamshire
Local history collection, Bancroft Library, Mile End
Reigate local studies collection, Guildford
Feltham local history collection
Twickenham local studies library
Kensal Green Cemetery Office Records
Eastbourne local history collection
Surrey County Record Office, Kingston
Society of Genealogists Library
Somerset Rural Life Museum, Glastonbury
York Herald, College of Arms

Grateful thanks are due to all who have helped me at the above locations, with special thanks to Miss Anne Milton, archivist at Walsingham, and to Dom Philip Jebb OSB, archivist of Downside Abbey.

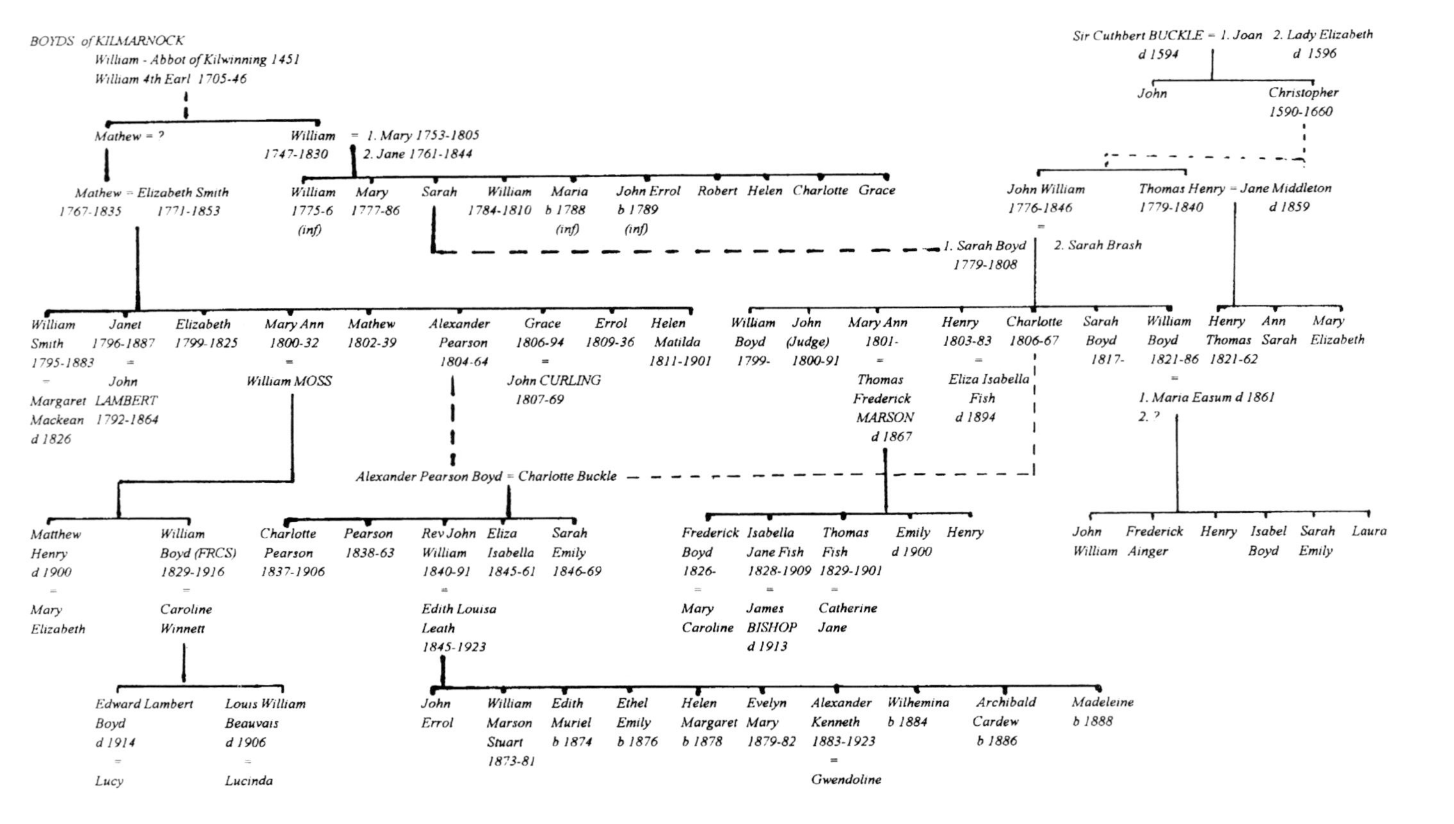

Family of CHARLOTTE PEARSON BOYD: benefactress

WALSINGHAM: DOWNSIDE AND THE BENEDICTINES

by Dom Aidan Bellenger, OSB

> Walsingham is a typical Norfolk village and Norfolk is unlike any other part of England. It is a county on its own with a charm all its own which, once it has laid hold of a man, has the power to drag him back from the remotest parts of the world. It is a county of sweeping horizons and deep silences, where the advance of the machine age has been halted and where the honk of the wild geese can still be heard as they thread their way through the evening sky. It is a windswept county of huge fields, vast soaring churches and small flint-built cottages. It is a county of great peace and quiet, where the widgeon feed on the marshes and the curlew swing through the empty air. And the people are like their county, silent, shrewd and suspicious of novelties, a people who like to "winter and summer" a man before they give him their trust and friendship, a trust and friendship which once given is never taken back.[1]

These words come from an early chapter of Bruno Scott James' autobiographical musings, characteristically entitled *Asking for Trouble*. Monsignor Bruno Scott James (1906-1984) was the first resident priest at the Slipper Chapel and he now lies buried at Downside in the shadow of the Abbey church. He is perhaps the latest of the many links between Walsingham and the Benedictines, especially the Benedictines of Downside Abbey in Somerset.

In its heyday in the Middle Ages, the Shrine at Walsingham was in the care of Augustinian Canons described by a recent monastic historian Professor C. H. Lawrence, as a "hybrid order of clerical monks".[2] The Canons attempted to initiate the apostolic life of the Early Church as described in the Acts of the Apostles but usually within a simpler framework of rules and regulations. The movement towards canonical foundations received substance and reform in the 12th century under the influence of the French abbeys of Arrouaise and Saint-Victor, Paris, and the first important Canon Regular house in England was the East Anglian community of St. Botolph at Colchester.[3] Eventually, numbered by foundations, the Augustinian Canons became the largest religious institution in Medieval England, with 274 houses, excluding alien priories, as compared to 219 Benedictine establishments.[4] In Norfolk there were 17 Augustinian foundations, many of them near the sea, and most founded in the late 12th and early 13th century. Creake was of abbatial status, the others, most of the small foundations were priories. Benedictines staffed the Cathedral Priory at Norwich and had an abbey at Holm dedicated to St. Benedict or Benet as well as priories at Wymondham (which became an abbey in 1448), Binham, Horsham St. Faith, Modeney, Molycourt and Mountjoy. Norwich Cathedral Priory had priory cells at Aldeby, Lynn and Yarmouth as well as at St. Leonard's in Norwich. The Cluniacs, a Benedictine reformed group of monasteries dependent on the Abbey of Cluny in Burgundy, had foundations in Bromholm, Castle Acre and Thetford. There were Benedictine nuns at Blackborough, Carrow (on the outskirts of Norwich) and Thetford. There were no Cistercian monks in the county but there were Cistercian nuns at Marham. There were also houses of Trinitarian canons, Gilbertines Premonstratensians and the various orders of Friars including a Franciscan Friary at Walsingham (established in 1347).[5]

The Augustinian Canons at Walsingham had a pilgrim centre of international importance but there were other places in the county which also attracted the pious. The great Cathedral church of Norwich lacked associations with any great saint but some visitors came to the Shrine of St. William of Norwich, a child said by some to have been murdered by Jews.[6] At Thetford there was a Marian shrine, the only one of importance in the county besides Walsingham, although many of the religious houses had a dedication to the Blessed Virgin Mary and represented her on their seals, often shown seated with the holy child on her knee.[7] At Thetford, about the middle of the 13th century, a local artisan, terminally ill, dreamt three times that the Blessed Virgin had appeared to him, and was told he would regain his health if the prior would build a Lady Chapel on the north side of the Chapel. The prior suggested a wooden building. The artisan, obviously a persuasive man, insisted on stone. When the work commenced an old statue of the Virgin was re-discovered and it was found to contain many precious relics as well as a letter saying that these objects had come from Jerusalem. When the relic-bearing image was placed in the choir miracles followed, not least of which was that the additional revenue helped to rebuild the choir of the church and the monastic refectory.[8] At Bromholm the crowds came in larger numbers, some of them taking it in with Walsingham itself, especially those who came as close to Walsingham as they could by sea.[9] The attraction at Bromholm was the cross, made of fragments of the true cross, brought to Bromholm from Constantinople in 1225 by an English priest. Many miracles were recorded and among those who came was Edward II in 1313. He had a special devotion to 'the glorious cross of Bromholm'. Its impact was said to be dramatic. In August 1401, Pope Boniface IX granted an indult to the Prior of Bromholm to hear the confessions and give absolution to the people who came to the church particularly as some, their sins being so heavy, were unable to look at the cross and sometimes became ill. The cross disappeared with the monastery at its dissolution in 1537.[10]

Henry VIII's reign brought an abrupt end to the religious life in Norfolk. All monastic houses were closed by the end of the 1530's, although in Mary Tudor's reign two Dominican nuns, formerly of Dartford in Kent, were resident in Walsingham.[11] Some shadowy religious life survived the Henrician reformation but its revival was slow.[12] By the end of the 16th century, as far as the Catholic authorities were concerned, England was missionary territory. In the first half of the 17th century the English Benedictines had reconstituted themselves as a missionary body and their three long-lived French-based priories at Douai, in Flanders, Dieulouard, in Lorraine, and Paris, along with their German abbey at Lambspring near Hildesheim, trained many generations of monk-missioners who joined their secular and Jesuit colleagues in England.[13] The community at Douai, dedicated to St. Gregory the Great, Apostle of the English, is the ancestor of modern-day Downside, Dieulouard (with St. Laurence as patron), of Ampleforth, and Paris (under the protection of the East Anglian, St. Edmund) of Douai Abbey at Woolhampton in Berkshire.

It was in 1603 that two of the earliest Benedictine missioners made their way to England and to Norfolk, probably indeed the first to arrive. Dom Thomas Preston and Dom Anselm Beech landed at Great Yarmouth and made their way to Caston, near Wymondham, where they were received in the house of Francis Woodhouse, whose wife was an open recusant. Here the two monks, both from Monte Cassino, where they had made their novitiate, encountered Dom Sigebert Buckley, once a monk of Mary Tudor's revised monastery at Westminster and a living link with pre-reformation Benedictinism. Buckley had long been a prisoner, most recently at Framlingham Castle in Suffolk from which he had been released on the accession of James I. He was to live on until 1610, long enough to 'aggregate' the new monks to the old monastic way.[14] Missionary monks had the prospect of an early death. Thomas Tunstal, ordained in 1609, was imprisoned under the alias of Richard Dyer in Newgate and Wisbech. He escaped from Wisbech, was recaptured and martyred at Norwich on 13th July 1616. He had become a Benedictine, perhaps by private vow, after his ordination and his head was placed after his death on St. Benedict's Gate at Norwich.[15]

Over the centuries that followed a number of Norfolk men entered the English Benedictine communities. The first were Maurus Atkins of Oatwell and John Mondeford or Mumford, both monks of St. Gregory's, Douai, professed in 1614. Another Norfolk-born monk, Cuthbert Wall or Marsh (aliases were frequently used to conceal identity), of Lambspring, came perilously near to death during the 'Popish Plot' of 1678 when he was tried for his priesthood. More recently, at the end of the 18th century, Benedict Deday, Norwich-born, became the first monk of St. Gregory's to make his vows after the community had settled in England following the French Revolution.[16] Some Benedictine missioners worked in Norfolk, but few records survive. It seems that monks supplied missions or chaplaincies at one time or another at Barmingham, Colkirk, Costessey and Oxburgh but there was no permanent Benedictine missionary presence until the end of the 19th century with the opening of a mission station at Wymondham and a chapel at Gillingham Hall served by the monks over the Suffolk border at Beccles.[17]

In the wake of the French Revolution, a community of Benedictine nuns from Montargis in France resided at Bodney Hall near Swaffham from 1793 to 1811. They took in English students and many English nuns eventually joined the community which was to find a more permanent home at Princethorpe in Warwickshire. It is now settled at Fernham near Oxford. The Bodney community had Our Lady as its abbess, in perpetuity, and was ruled by a prioress. This system, introduced at the time of the community's foundation in 1630, was not only a Marian devotion but an attempt to avoid the all-too common fate of convents of the period in having a non-resident, commendatory superior, an absentee, often a lay person, who appropriated the revenues of the community.[18]

The life as lived at Bodney would be far nearer to the type of "normal" Benedictine life which converts like Charlotte Boyd (1837-1906) looked for in the Catholic Church than the still mission-based monks of the English Benedictine Congregation in the closing years of the 19th century.[19] It was in an enclosed community, the English convent in Bruges, dedicated to Nazareth, an English exiled community of Augustinians, that Charlotte to whose context and to whose Benedictine connections we must now turn, was received into the Catholic Church on 22nd September 1894.[20] It was during a time when, having failed in her attempts to buy the ruins of Walsingham Priory she was now turning her attention to the Houghton Pilgrim Chapel. If she had not been converted it seems she most probably would have handed the property over to Church of England owners. Charlotte Boyd, an independent lady of means, was much involved in High Church activities during a time when Anglo-Catholicism was gaining in strength and confidence. In 1850 she had been struck by the ruins of the once-great abbey at Glastonbury that she determined to dedicate her life to 'restoration' of the Church as it had once been. In 1875 she made possible the foundation of the English Abbey Restoration Trust, dedicated to reclaiming ecclesiastical properties from secular hands. Miss Boyd's most noteworthy purchase was probably in 1892 when she acquired the remains of West Malling Abbey in Kent which she had visited as early as 1874. Malling had originally been founded in about 1090 by Gundulf, Bishop of Rochester, as a monastery for nuns, and had been dissolved in 1538. Miss Boyd gave the abbey to the Anglican community at Feltham in Middlesex which had been founded in 1868 under the influence of Father Ignatius of Llanthony.[21]

In 1861 as a deacon in London's docklands, not then as decorous as now, Joseph Leycester Lyne, began wearing a habit and announced he had 'revived' the Order of St. Benedict in the Church of England. Calling himself Ignatius of Jesus, under the unlikely patronage of Ignatius Loyola, he lived for brief periods at different places including Claydon, Suffolk (1862), Norwich (1863) and Laleham, Middlesex (1867) before migrating to Llanthony in the Black Mountains of South Wales. His was an eclectic monasticism and he effectively broke with the Church of England when he was ordained to the priesthood by an Old Catholic in 1897. "His memory" according to Peter Anson, "will live rather as one of the greatest mission preachers and orators of the 19th century than as a Benedictine monk." Nevertheless, at his death, in 1908 some of his followers joined the monastic community at Caldey Island from which sprang both Prinknash Abbey, and its dependents, and Elmore Abbey, the first Catholic, the second Anglican.[22] Father Ignatius' vacillation on becoming a 'Roman' Catholic reflected a view within the Anglican church that Catholicism would be achieved without 'submission' to Rome. Indeed many thought that some sort of 'corporate' reunion was a strong possibility and a desirable option. The debates following the defections from the Church of England on the combined issues of 'Authority' and women's ordination in recent years reflect the same concerns. Charlotte Boyd's circle were gradually to move Romewards but many of the young clergy and laymen, called, as they saw it, to the religious life did not think they could find an obvious home in the rather inbred and parish-centred English Benedictine monasteries.

In the late 19th century the idea of a return to traditional Benedictine monasticism was making an increasing impact. Monasticism seemed, in its purist form, an antidote to the secularism and materialism which had already led (through their ally nationalism) to a *Külturkampf* in Germany, a *risorgimento* in Italy and an increasingly anti-clerical Third Republic in France. In Germany the abbey of Beuron was restored in 1863 by the brothers Maurus and Placid Wolter whose *Principles of Monasticism* inspired a new congregation of monasteries including Maredsous in Belgium (1872) and Erdington in the outskirts of Birmingham (1876). Maredsous, founded with money from the Desclée family, famous for their liturgical publications, had acquired, under its abbots Hildebrand de Hemptinne (1890-1909) and the anglophone, Dublin-born, Columba Marmion (1909-23) a great spiritual reputation, which made it a mecca for wavering Anglo-Catholics. It was not surprising that Charlotte Boyd felt inspired to offer an endowment for some Masses in 1893 that God's will be done in England. In Italy the reforms initiated at Benedict's own monastery at Subiaco in 1851 were influential in the foundation of Ramsgate Abbey in Kent where a full Benedictine observance was probably in place in England for the first time since the Reformation. In France the monastery of Solesmes, restored in 1833 by Abbot Prosper Guéranger established a reputation for monasticism and for the chant which made it of much more than national importance.[23]

In time, all these movements were influencing the English Benedictines and following a visitation from Rome, the English monks adapted new constitutions (in 1899) which while leaving intact the missionary work of the Congregation, re-ordered the previously monolithic structure into the traditional abbatial government. This change owed much to the energies of Edmund Ford, Prior and later Abbot of Downside,[24] with whom Charlotte Boyd negotiated the transfer of the Houghton Chapel to the Downside conventus in 1896.

This context of an increasing Benedictine awareness of its monastic identity and its great medieval past - also reflected in the writings of Abbot (later

Cardinal) Gasquet on monastic history[25] - is important in understanding why Charlotte Boyd turned to the English monks. But if context is important Miss Boyd's individual contacts are perhaps even more so. In 1960, in correspondence with the then Abbot of Downside, Christopher Butler, H. M. Gillett attempted to piece together the chronological, personal and monastic story of the Downside connection with Walsingham. Among the personalities he mentions are Henry Feasey, Henry Worth, Ethelbert Taunton and Bede Camm.[26]

Henry Feasey, "for years an ardent supporter of Father Ignatius of Llanthony" was converted to Catholicism by Miss Boyd's example and was received at Downside in June 1898. He joined the monastery at Ramsgate on the death of his mother in 1899. He was an autodidact but of great learning, elected a Fellow of the Royal Historical Society in 1903, and ordained deacon before his death in 1908.[27] His *Monasticism: What is it?* publication in 1898, is dedicated to the Downside community. He contributed, in the same year, two articles in *The Downside Review*, one on Malling, the other on Walsingham. In 1901 he published his *History of Our Ladye of Walsingham* with notes by Henry Curties on the "Pilgrim Chapel" at "Houghton-le-Dale" and a three-line letter of support for his "proposal and work" by Bishop Riddell. Feasey hoped that Walsingham could be crucial in the "golden chain of prayer" which would "draw England back to the Catholic Faith." In particular, he hoped that the Pilgrim Chapel, now in "Catholic hands" could be put back in use.[28]

Henry George Worth (1852-1912) was a curate (along with Reginald Camm) at St. Agnes, Kennington Park and was (also with Camm) an honorary Chaplain at Miss Boyd's orphanage at Kilburn in North London. He was a dedicated student of liturgy, plainsong and monastic history and it was during a visit to the Benedictine monastery at Stanbrook (for women) in October 1895 "to hear the chant", much influenced by Solesmes, that he was received into the church. His chronic ill-health did not prevent him from collating many liturgical manuscripts. On his death he left his library to Stanbrook.[29]

Ethelbert Taunton (1857-1907) was a boy at Downside in the 1860's but like Worth suffered from ill-health. This prevented him from joining the monastery but he was ordained, as an Oblate of St. Charles, in 1883. It was in Bruges that he began his career as a prolific and polemical writer eulogising the Benedictines in his *English Black Monks* (1897) and demonising the Society of Jesus in his *History of the English Jesuits* (1901). His obituarist in *The Downside Review* wrote that he had "a straight-forward and ruthless honesty, which was not always appreciated."[30] Taunton's acquaintance with Miss Boyd, which led to helping him out financially (chronic insolvency went with his health),[31] probably introduced her to the key figures in the Downside 'reform' movement like Prior Ford and Gilbert Dolan (1853-1914), a literary man and a historian, with a keen architectural interest.[32] Thomas Garner, once Bodley's partner, and the architect of the choir of Downside Abbey was the consultant architect at the Slipper Chapel at the time of Miss Boyd's purchase and emergency restoration.

Reginald Bede Camm[33] was known to Miss Boyd long before he joined Downside. Bede Camm (1864-1942), educated at Westminster and Keble College, Oxford, was the first of her circle to become a Catholic, in 1890. He joined Maredsous and was ordained priest in 1895 moving to Erdington soon after. In 1913 he was affiliated to Downside. He was a significant martyrologist and a devoted antiquarian. His handsome *Forgotten Shrines* (London, 1910) remembered the world of country house Catholicism retreating in the face of encroaching suburbia. Camm, like all the Boyd circle were keen on the physical links with the Catholic past. For them reclaiming the building was almost like reclaiming the soul, aesthetic and religious sensibility being closely allied. Reparation for the past could then be tangibly called-up. For others it was action, pilgrimages rather than pilgrim-sites, renewal rather than reflection, which attracted. Father Philip Fletcher (1848-1928) and his Guild of Our Lady of Ransom which made much of the Pilgrimage of 19th/20th August 1897 was delighted with the new Lynn Chapel and made little of the Slipper Chapel in his memoirs.[34]

This would have probably pleased the then Bishop of Northampton. Arthur Riddell seems to have been the most implacable opponent to opening the Slipper Chapel for even private use. Born at York in 1836 he, too, was a Downside old boy, at the school from 1841 to 1851, before proceeding to Ushaw from where he was ordained priest. Most of his life as a priest was spent at Hull before he was consecrated as Bishop of Northampton on 9th June 1880.[35] In 1895, writing to Miss Boyd on 13th August he confided that he would like to place "a good missionary priest at the Slipper Chapel" who "might in time establish little missions at Dereham, Fakenham and Wells."[36] He also said that he wanted to visit the Chapel with the Rev. George Wrigglesworth (1851-1900), the priest at King's Lynn.[37] Although Miss

Boyd thought the Bishop had an aversion to all religious, especially Benedictines, and this seems confirmed by his negative attitude to the establishment of a (Downside) Benedictine presence at Cambridge,[38] also in his diocese, it seems most likely that the development of the Shrine at King's Lynn, an established mission, was the real cause of the prohibition. "There is only one pilgrimage approved by me, that to the Shrine of Our Lady of Walsingham at Lynn. I cannot," he wrote to Prior Ford on 28th May 1900, "approve of any other."[39] Money, as so often in church matters, may have been the heart of the matter. Father Philip Fletcher remembered seeing a pleading advertisement, "Help! Help! My church is falling!" This was from George Wrigglesworth. In time a new church was built and Fletcher and Wrigglesworth sought to revive the Walsingham pilgrimage - with the Lynn church as the centrepiece.[40] Many bishops of the time, including the veteran Benedictine Ullathorne, while admiring monks in monasteries thought they had little role to play in the parishes.[41]

In June 1903 Miss Boyd had suggested that Downside should offer the property to the diocese and indeed described Walsingham as "only one of her fads,"[42] but it was not until the 1920s that the question was raised at the Downside Chapter of alienating the property.[43] Bishop Dudley Charles Cary Elwes was keen on the transfer, as he revealed in a letter to Abbot Cuthbert Butler in February 1922[44] but it was only in 1931 that the Slipper Chapel ceased to be Downside property, following the decision of the Downside Chapter to pass it over in 1930.[45]

The Northampton authorities reacted by this time to the growing success of the Anglican Shrine under the inspiration of the Reverend Alfred Hope Patten. In 1925 there had been a correspondence between the Abbot of Downside and Hope Patten, of a cordial nature, which suggested that prayers could be said by Anglican pilgrims outside the Slipper Chapel but not in it.[46] Ecumenical relations were strained and this seemingly small gesture was frowned on by the parish priest of Fakenham. With the return to devotion at Walsingham itself, the time was approaching for a renewed Roman Catholic presence. This was symbolised by the proper restoration of the Chapel. It was not a little ironic that the first resident administrator of the Catholic Shrine had strong Downside connections.

Bruno Scott James was an independent-minded, freelance priest, who though he was what some might have considered eccentric, contributed greatly to the life of the church. His education was erratic but his years spent as a monk at Pershore, an Anglican Benedictine foundation, and abroad gave him a rare, somewhat detached, insight into the contemporary Catholic Church. It was at the Slipper Chapel that he decided to become a Catholic. Turning from Anglo-Catholicism was to be a difficult decision, saying goodbye to so much he liked.

> One day, driven to the verge of desperation by the awful choice that seemed to lie ahead of me, I walked out to the Slipper Chapel and, having obtained the key from the custodian, threw myself on my knees and implored God to give me the grace to follow his will whatever the cost might be and wherever it might lead me. I then vowed, hardly realising what I said, that if Our Lady would obtain from her Son this grace for me I would devote my life to her service at Walsingham. Although I did not realise it at the time, that was, I am sure, a turning point in my life. I think that in my sub-conscious mind I had already made my decision, and all I was praying for was the strength to follow it. Three months later - three of the most painful and agonising months I have ever known - I was received into the Catholic Church.[47]

He was an inveterate visitor of monasteries and had a particularly soft spot for Downside.

> I confess that I had hitherto held the half-baked opinion - now happily less common than it was - that the monks at Downside led an easy, not to say relaxed, life. Of course nothing could be further from the truth. I am privileged with the friendship of monks and their communities all over Europe, but I know of no community where the life is more exacting than at Downside. This is not obvious as first because, if the community has any fault, it is that of self-deprecation. The monks are all of them rather too prone to hide their light and disguise the hardship of their life under a façade of something rather akin to flippancy. But I find this infinitely preferable to the terrifying smugness and self-satisfaction too often evident amongst monks living a superficially harder life. Loving the Carthusians as I do, my hair always begins to stand on end when a Carthusian monk starts off with the cliché, "We say it in all humility", for I know perfectly well what to expect. It will be

a long discourse on the perfection of their life. Neither are the Trappists exempt from this defect, unfortunately. It is true that by the very nature of their rather special work the monks of Downside have rather more contact with the world than would otherwise be desirable for a monk, and it would be asking too much of human nature to expect that none of them should ever be affected by this. The wonder is that so few are, and that so many are able to lead an heroic life of prayer and union with God under these difficult circumstances. An endearing feature of the community is that none of the monks take each other in the least seriously. Certain of them are very distinguished scholars with European reputations in their particular line, but none of their brethren take any notice of this. What is even more endearing, they do not seem to think anything of it themselves.[48]

At his first Mass in Rome, at St. Anselmo, the Benedictine College, following his ordination at St. John Lateran which came after a period at the Beda College, he was assisted by a Downside monk, Wilfrid Passmore (later Abbot) and Mgr. Charles Duchemin, Rector of the Beda, a Downside old boy. Immediately after his ordination he was appointed by Bishop Youens as first resident parish priest of Walsingham and custodian of the Shrine since the Reformation. The Slipper Chapel had already been restored by Mgr. Harold Squirrell (1872-1962) of Norwich very much to Scott James' taste.

Interior of Slipper Chapel - 1936.

The stone altar was clothed with a fine silk frontal and the small tabernacle for the Blessed Sacra-

> ment was covered with a veil of pure cloth of gold. Behind the altar a fine reredos had been set, carved, painted and gilded in the medieval tradition of local craftsmen. The statue of Our Lady of Walsingham, which was the Shrine, stood on a carved wooden pedestal against the wall on the left of the Chapel, with a soaring canopy of gilded and painted wood over it. The statue itself had been designed by Professor Tristram from the replica on the ancient seal of Walsingham. It was a striking statue, full of character, carved in wood and painted in subdued colours. But it was too austere for tastes formed on the mass-produced *bondieuserie* of the Place S. Sulpice, or on what is called Catholic repository art. It has now been removed for one of more sentimental appeal.[49]

The problem faced by the newly-ordained priest was not the chapel but the lack of pilgrims. The National Pilgrimage of 1934 which celebrated the opening of the Chapel seemed at the time to be a one-off. I will let Scott James himself describe the gradual build-up of the pilgrimage in his years, those which went up to 1943 when Bishop Parker succeeded the gentle Youens.

> The first pilgrimage to come after my arrival was led by Bishop Craven, then Father Craven of the Crusade of Rescue. It amounted to some hundred persons and seemed enormous, but the time was to come when I would think nothing of a thousand. At first the pilgrims came in dribs and drabs. Not until the middle of my second year at Walsingham did they begin to come in real crowds. From then until the war, I was busy preaching sometimes as often as eight times a day and hearing confessions not infrequently from six in the evening until midnight. Some would come on foot, some by bicycle, some by special trains and very many by buses. They came from all over the country and sometimes from France, Italy and Belgium. By the outbreak of the war a conservative estimate of the numbers was fifty thousand a year, but they were difficult to assess because so very many came on their own and went away without leaving any record. Private cars were arriving all day. By the middle of my third year there I began to build a sacristy and a chapel in honour of the Holy Ghost. Somewhere to keep the vestments and a place for the many visiting priests to vest for Mass

were essential, as also was another chapel for visiting priests to say Mass. When it became known that I intended to build on to the Slipper Chapel, there was an immediate uproar amongst those, mostly Anglicans and archaeologists, who thought the Slipper Chapel too perfect to be touched. Every post brought letters of protest, some anonymous and one, strongly worded, from the Anglican Dean of Norwich, no doubt written in the utmost good faith. To the Dean I simply replied that when the Slipper Chapel was in Anglican hands and used as a barn for the storage of crops I could understand that there would not have been any compelling need to build, but now that it had come back to our hands and was being used once again for Divine Worship some development was necessary and inevitable. I understand that this letter of mine was widely quoted as a blatant example of Roman Catholic intolerance. In fact, the whole addition was so planned as to detract as little as possible from the fine proportions of the original.[50]

There was also the possibility of wider pastoral work. He left much of the work of organising the pilgrimage to his pilgrimage Secretary, Claude Fisher.

During the second year a side of my work began to develop which appealed to me very much more than the organised pilgrimages. It began with my preaching every day from the steps of the Slipper Chapel to any who might be passing. Even when there was no formal pilgrimage, a large crowed overflowing on to the road never failed to collect. Nearly always the crowd contained persons in need of help; quite often men and women who had lapsed for years from their faith, to find it again at the feet of Our Lady at the Slipper Chapel. From this developed my plan of giving retreats to men, so that before long there were young men of every kind and class coming to Walsingham to learn how to be still and know God. Since my house had only one spare room, I built for them at the end of my garden small one-roomed houses or huts of cedar wood. With their high-pitched shingle roofs they looked not unlike tiny alpine cottages. Within there was a bunk, a bookshelf, a table and a chair. It was my dream that Walsingham should become not only a place of pilgrimage, but also a power-house of prayer - the two do not necessarily go together. It was for a group of young men who came to Walsingham regularly for this purpose that I wrote my first book, *The One Thing Necessary*. I wrote it at their request after the war had broken out, so that while they were fighting they might have something they could keep in their pockets and read at odd moments to remind them of what they had learned at Walsingham.[51]

In the midst of all the activity there was always laughter.

Once, a very important ecclesiastic who was leading a pilgrimage disappeared. Frantic search eventually revealed that he had got locked into a necessary, but not very commodious or comfortable, room in the local hostelry. Mine host refused to let us break the door down; there was nothing for it but to rescue the unfortunate though none-the-less important ecclesiastic through the rather restricted space of the window. Anyone who has had the experience of trying to extract a rather portly ecclesiastic from a small window in the upper story of an inn, and then convey him to the ground by means of a rickety ladder, with a large crowd watching the spectacle from the courtyard below, will sympathise with the difficulties and hazards involved. I regret to say that the language of the ecclesiastic on this occasion was not precisely what my mother had taught me to expect from a clergyman.[52]

Father Bruno Scott James.

On his departure from Walsingham, which included a three year stay near Downside, Scott James began a variety of apostolates which culminated in the foundation of the John Henry Newman College, a hall of residence for students at the University of Naples. In his affectionate tribute in *The Tablet* for 7th April 1984, Bishop Gordon Wheeler remembered Scott James' "unusual but fruitful apostolate" at Walsingham:-

This rather eccentric priest enveloped in a black cloak, his head shorn, and with a Siamese cat perched on his shoulder, squatting on the steps of the

Slipper Chapel as he poured out pearls of patristic wisdom, was an inspiration to many. He had a great gift of prayer himself and was able to communicate this to others.[53]

Any pilgrim centre is always a palimpsest of past and present. The Slipper Chapel's survival as the centrepiece of the Catholic Shrine owes much to Charlotte Boyd and her Benedictine beneficiaries and to its surprisingly numerous monastic connections. I hope I have put them into some sort of context.

REFERENCES

Abbreviations:

DAA Downside Abbey Archives (Walsingham Files)
DR The Downside Review
James B. S. James, Asking for Trouble, London, 1962.
VCH The Victoria History of the County of Norfolk, Volume 2, ed. by W. Page, London (1906).

1. James, p. 48.
2. C. H. Lawrence, Medieval Monasticism, London (1984) p.137.
3. ibid., p.140.
4. ibid., p.141.
5. VCH, pp.315-7, For the Walsingham Franciscans, see p.435.
6. D. H. Farmer, Oxford Dictionary of Saints, Third Edition, Oxford (1992) p.496.
7. VCH, pp.315-466 passim.
8. ibid., pp.364-5.
9. L. E. Whatmore, Highway to Walsingham, Walsingham (1973) pp.72-3.
10. VCH, pp.361-2.
11. Whatmore, op. cit., pp. 105-6.
12. J. J. Scarisbrick, The Reformation and the English People, Oxford (1984).
13. D. Lunn, The English Benedictines, London (1980).
14. ibid., p.28.
15. G. Anstruther, The Seminary Priests 2, The Early Stuarts 1603-1659, Great Wakering, (1975), pp.324-5.
16. G. Dolan, "Chapters in the History of the English Benedictine Missions, 2, Norfolk," DR 15 (1896), pp.162-71.
17. ibid.
18. D. A. Bellenger, The French Exiled Clergy on the British Isles after 1789, Bath, (1986) pp.90-93.
19. For the English Benedictines in the Nineteenth Century, see D. Rees (ed.), Monks of England, London (1997).
20. For Charlotte Boyd, see essay by E. M. Hostler on this volume and also by the same author, "Charlotte Boyd - Some notes on her life", in a supplement to The Messenger (Catholic League) 257 (1996).

21. A. M. Oakley, Malling Abbey, Malling (1990).
22. P. F. Anson, The Benedictines of Caldey, London (1939) pp.xxvii- xxviii. For Father Ignatius see D. Attwater, Father Ignatius of Llanthony, London (1931).
23. D. Rees, "The Benedictine Revival in the Nineteenth Century", in D. H. Farmer, ed., Benedict's Disciples, Leominster (1980) pp.282-307.
24. G. B. Hicks, Hugh Edmund Ford, London (1947) especially pp.53-8 for his work at Beccles.
25. S. Leslie, Cardinal Gasquet, London (1953).
26. DAA, H. M. Gillett to Abbot Christopher Butler, 27 April 1960.
27. DR 27 (1908) p.93. Obituary Notice of Dom Philibert Feasey. See also Album Benedictinum, Rome, 1910, under Ramsgate.
28. H. Feasey, History of Our Ladye of Walsingham, London (1901) pp.6-7.
29. DR 32 (1913) p.95 Obituary Notice of Henry George Worth.
30. DR 26 (1907) p.223.
31. ibid.
32. For Gilbert Dolan see DR 33 (1914) pp.252-4.
33. For Bede Camm, see D. A. Bellenger, "Dom Bede Camm (1864-1942), Monastic Martyrologist", in Studies in Church History 30 (1993), pp.371-81.
34. P. Fletcher, Reflections of a Ransomer, London (1928) pp.85-8.
35. DR 26 (1907) pp.313-4 for an Obituary of Bishop Riddell.
36. DAA, Bishop Riddell to Charlotte Boyd, 13 August 1895.
37. ibid. Father Wrigglesworth was a native of Hull, ordained in 1883. He had gone to King's Lynn in 1887, opening a school in 1894 and opening a new church on 2 June 1897. The foundation stone had been laid by Bishop Riddell on 29 September 1896. A Rescript of 6th February 1897 had restored the Shrine of Our Lady of Walsingham to this Church in Kings' Lynn (Information from Pamphlets issued in 1997 to mark the Church's centenary).
38. P. Jebb, "Benet House, Cambridge", E. B. C. History Symposium 15 (1997), pp.48-9.
39. DAA, Bishop Riddell to Hugh Edmund Ford, 28 May 1900.
40. Fletcher, op. cit., pp.85-6.
41. D. Rees, Monks of England, op. cit., for background.
42. DAA, Charlotte Boyd to Hugh Edmund Ford, 2 January 1903.
43. DAA, 14 May 1922. Chapter votes No to Alienation.
44. ibid., Dudley Charles Cary-Elwes to Cuthbert Butler, 16 February 1922.
45. Letter of Abbot Charles Fitzgerald-Lombard of Downside in Walsingham 100 Years Souvenir Programme, Walsingham, 1997, p.12.
46. DAA, Alfred Hope Patten to Cuthbert Butler, 8 August 1925 and Cuthbert Butler to Alfred Hope Patten, 12 August 1925.
47. James, p.54.
48. ibid., pp.109-10.
49. ibid., p.121.
50. ibid., pp.122-3.
51. ibid., p.124.
52. ibid., pp.125-6.
53. The Tablet, 7 April 1984, pp.337-8. The present author served Mgr Scott James' Requiem Mass at Downside.

THE RED MOUNT CHAPEL, KING'S LYNN

by Dr. Paul Richards

This fascinating and unusual medieval religious building stands just inside the former town defences in parkland known today as The Walks. It is a familiar, much drawn and photographed landmark but rarely visited in the late 20th century. In 1962 Pevsner described the Red Mount Chapel as "one of the strangest Gothic churches in England". It was in fact built in the 1480s as a wayside chapel for pilgrims travelling through Lynn to the famous Shrine of Our Lady at Walsingham in North Norfolk. The name 'Red Mount Chapel' could derive from its red brick or from 'Rood Mount' (in Anglo-Saxon 'rood' is a cross and one may have topped the building).

Why did so many thousands of pilgrims en route for Walsingham every year come first to Lynn? As important in the Middle Ages as Liverpool was to become in the Industrial Revolution, it was a boom town from 1100, with access to a wide hinterland via the Ouse River system by 1300. This Wash seaport faced Europe across the North Sea and coastal traffic linked it to London and northern Britain.

Lynn's medieval merchants had ships to hire. Pilgrims from the Baltic or the Netherlands or Scotland probably formed parties for the long sea journey to Norfolk. They disembarked at the Purfleet, the town's harbour, and started their return journey from the same place. In the early 20th century, pilgrim badges were retrieved by boys from this river and the Lynn Museum contains the collection.

The main overland route or way to Walsingham was that due north from London but other pilgrims approached Lynn from the north and west on rough roads. Whether arriving in the town by ship or foot, there was still another 23 miles to trek before reaching Walsingham. Margery Kempe (c1373-c1440) of Lynn went to Walsingham on her way to Norwich and Ipswich in 1433. So, too, did English medieval kings who felt obliged to display their devotion to Our Lady at the Shrine. In 1498 Henry VII journeyed to Lynn with his family and large retinue, staying at the Augustinian Friary, then setting out for Walsingham.

Pilgrims travelling to Walsingham via Lynn were resting in the town and thanking God for safe passage before the 1480s, probably on the site of the

Red Mount Chapel. We know that the 'Gild of Our Lady on the Mount', founded in 1329, had a chapel here. This must now be the lower chapel embraced by the mound. Did growing pilgrim traffic jog the Prior of St. Margaret's Church at Lynn into building a new wayside chapel in the 1480s? Such a project not only demonstrated his devotion to Our Lady but significantly increased the depressed income of the Priory Church through the offerings of pilgrims.

William Spynke is the Prior in this story. He commissioned Robert Currance to commence the building in 1483 without having first secured the consent of the Mayor and Commons. This was public land and work was brought to a halt! Not until 1485 did the Mayor and Commons agree to grant Mr Currance a licence to build a chapel on "Ladye Hylle" providing not too much grazing land was taken up.

The Red Mount Chapel (above ground) is of two storeys and an octagon of red brick in the perpendicular style with buttresses and stone windows. Two staircases run around the space between this outer wall and an inner masonry core. There are two chapels. The lower must be that of the early 14th century already mentioned. The mound in which it is concealed was no doubt raised when the upper chapel was constructed. The upper chapel is cruciform in shape, of stone, and stands on top of the octagon. Its ceiling of fine fan tracery is similar to that found in King's College Chapel at Cambridge. We know that the upper chapel was completed by 1485 because Lynn's Mayor gave a pair of candlesticks for the altar in that year. Between the two chapels is a small cell which may have served as a vestry for the priest in charge.

Prior Spynke was a Benedictine. It is thus interesting to speculate whether the design of the Red Mount Chapel has its origins in the preferences of that order. This seems to be confirmed by references in Hillen (1907) to a similar building at Amboise in France and in Parkin (1762) to a Greek monastery. Details of the interior of the Red Mount Chapel can be found in Taylor's *Antiquities of Kings Lynn* (1844). What is certain is that Prior Spynke was expecting his new building to attract people. The double staircases and separate doors for entry and exit tell of his purpose to expedite the flow of pilgrims on their Walsingham way.

The new Red Mount Chapel did not enjoy a long life as a wayside chapel for pilgrims. An anonymous Lynn chronicler talks vividly of the changes brought about by the English Reformation unleashed by Henry VIII. In 1536 "pylgiymes and idolytrye" were "forbyden" and the town friaries dissolved along with the Priory at St. Margaret's. In Walsingham a crowd resisted the closure of the abbey and, for their part in this act of defiance, William Guisborough and his father from Lynn were executed. There does not seem to be a great deal of evidence that the pilgrimage to Walsingham or devotion to Our Lady were in decline by the early 16th century. At the Red Mount Chapel in 1509 offerings totalled £16 10s. which was a considerable sum for the time.

Harrod (1874) suggests that the Red Mount Chapel had a roof (over the upper chapel) and this was dismantled about 1571 to supply building materials for the Corporation's main landing stage by the Ouse. The Mayor and burgesses do not, however, continue with the destruction of their new property, perhaps through the intervention of the Church. The lower chapel was used as a reservoir by 1578. The upper chapel appears to have been converted into a study for the vicar of St. Margaret's (1586-1617). In 1642 five barrels of gunpowder were stored at 'St. Mary Mount' and during the Civil War it was called 'Mount Fort'. It may have been used to house plague victims, almost certainly in the 1660s (a chimney was inserted at some point).

It is fortunate that the Red Mount Chapel was not pillaged for building materials to any extent after its desecration and closure in the 1530s. It was nevertheless allowed to fall into decay in the course of the 18th century. Then, in 1783, the Corporation resolved to repair the structure for use by "students of navigation in this borough", though little or nothing appears to have been done. By this time the area had been laid out as a new park or walk for Lynn's 'high caste folk' and the Red Mount Chapel was seen as a picturesque addition. As a Norfolk tour guide by Beatniffe (1795) observed:

> About half way between the South and East Gates, stand the remains of an ancient oratory, an odd sort of building, with several vaults and cavities under ground over which are some dark cells for the priests to take confessions in, and above them a small chapel in the figure of a cross, arched above, and enriched with carvings; it is dedicated to the blessed Virgin and commonly called "The Lady's", or "The Red Mount", whither the Romish penitents, in their pilgrimage to the holy wells and monastery of Our Lady at Walsingham, used to resort, and perform their devotions.

Engraving of the Red Mount Chapel - 1783.

William Richards, in his *History of Lynn* (1812), refers to the Red Mount Chapel as a "unique structure" but "this curious building is in a dilapidate state" and he calls for repairs and preservation. It remained in a perilous state and the lower chapel was being used as a stable according to a *Norfolk Tour* (1829). However, the joint exertions of the Reverends Edwards and Blencowe had already resulted in a successful subscription to enable extensive repairs to be undertaken (1828), and this restoration was complete by 1830.

REFERENCES

R. Beatniffe, The Norfolk Tour, Norwich (1795).

M. Gallyon, Margery Kempe of Lynn and Medieval England, Norwich (1995).

H. Harrod, Report on the Deeds and Records of the Borough of King's Lynn, King's Lynn (1874).

H. Hillen, History of the Borough of King's Lynn, Norwich (1907).

C. Parkin, The Topography of Freebridge Hundred and Half in the Country of Norfolk, London (1762).

N. Pevsner, The Buildings of England: North - West and South Norfolk, Harmondsworth (1977).

P. Richards, King's Lynn, Phillimore (1990).

W. Richards, The History of King's Lynn, Lynn (1812).

J. Stacy, A General History of the County of Norfolk or Norfolk Tour, Norwich (1829).

W. Taylor, The Antiquities of King's Lynn, King's Lynn (1844).

SOCIAL CONDITIONS IN VICTORIAN WALSINGHAM

by Howard Fears

History has been defined as "the ability to imagine yourself into the situation of someone different from you in the past."[1]

Queen Victoria came to the throne in June 1837 and after a reign of more than 63 years she died in January 1901. Her reign saw the population of England and Wales more than double[2] during a time of growth, experiment and change and of increased longevity and decreased mortality. One might also describe Victorian rural life as so dull that the highlight of the year was the School Inspector's annual visit. So to see whether Little Walsingham (hereinafter referred to as Walsingham) fits either description we will examine social and economic life in the village during Queen Victoria's reign as an intermingling of national and local events. In practical terms we will try and analyse a number of pertinent topics to produce our over-all broad picture.

Our first topic will be **demography**, a dull-sounding subject but an understanding of which is vital to a realisation of what happened in those years, bearing in mind that history is not simply a list of facts: it is the story we can draw from them.

Figures for England and Wales show a national population growth between 1841 and 1901 from 16 million to 32½ million, i.e. an increase of more than 100%. By comparison, Walsingham had 1,091 people in 1841, a peak of 1,141 in 1851 but only 924 in 1891, i.e. a decrease against the national average of 58%.

The early 19th century was noted for its high infant mortality: nationally 10% to 20% died under one year of age and 40% under age 20. Walsingham Burial Registers[3] show that even as late as 1864-72, when the average annual number of burials was 22, of these 36% were children 5 years and under, although the 1864 local Scarlet Fever epidemic produced a high level of deaths amongst Walsingham children, such as four infants in one family, and at one time seven awaiting burial. By the century's end, however, average family size decreased from six to three children and killer infections such as tuberculosis were gradually overcome. Indeed, the decline in infant mortality contributed most to population growth.

Population in Little Walsingham 1841-1891

YEAR	TOTAL (Male and Female)	of whom 9 and under	10 - 19	70 and over
1841	1091	275	222	62
1851	1141	262	259	65
1861	1050	236	207	50
1871	1016	233	185	62
1881	1010	247	219	53
1891	924	n/a	n/a	n/a

(Source: Walsingham Enumerators' Schedules 1841-1891; Norfolk Records Office.)

Why, then, the decline in rural population, and, typically, in Walsingham? The answer is migration, i.e. moving out from the countryside to urban areas, including London and the industrial regions or emigration, i.e. leaving England altogether for Canada, America, Australia and South Africa. Between 1841 and 1901 approximately four million[4] moved from rural England to the towns, and large numbers emigrated, in the end this left an unbalanced, typically ageing rural population.

Next a quick glance at survival and contingency. The economic uplift of the 1840's railway mania led to boom and subsequent financial panic. 1846-50 and 1868-73 have been described as Golden Ages for farmers, but of more significance was the Great Depression lasting for more than 20 years between 1873 and 1896, resulting in many arable farmers being destroyed, causing agricultural rents to fall and country estates and their owners to be broken. Throughout Victoria's reign food stuff prices varied enormously. For example, after the outbreak of the Crimean War (1852-54) dairy product prices rose by 250% (cheese from 7d. to 1s. 6d. per lb.) whilst wheat prices halved between 1871 and 1900.

Typical Weekly Wage Rates:
Fully Employed Norfolk Agricultural Labourers

1837	10s 4d	(i.e. 52p)
1851	9s 0d - 9s 7d	(i.e. 48p)
1860	11s 1d - 11s 7d	(i.e. 58p)
1870s	12s	(i.e. 60p)
1880s	13s 9d	(i.e. 69p)
1890s	15s 1d	(i.e. 75p)

The wages of agricultural labourers remained low for most of the period. For them, the real problem was that full time work was available for only one in three, with another third underemployed, liable to be turned away when bad weather or lack of work made them unnecessary. The remaining third was effectively unemployed except at harvest and a few peak periods when farmers needed every pair of hands they could hire. Then every labourer, wives and even quite young children worked every available minute. But for most of the year the labourer's poor earnings had to be stretched and when that failed all that remained for the labourer and his family was recourse to friends, then the Poor Law Guardians leading finally to the hated work-house.[5]

The largest Walsingham male employment group in Victoria's reign was the agricultural labourers, totalling from 37% to 44% of the male workforce. But whilst men in their 20s and 30s might be best for hard agricultural labour, in practice such labourers varied in age between 10 and 85. Walsingham census figures reveal that in 1841 more labourers were aged between 70 and 80 than between 50 and 59.

A labourer's life gave little opportunity for active leisure and young ambitious men failing to migrate or emigrate might be seduced by the Army Recruiting Sergeant's attractive uniform and the promise of one shilling per day. During the Crimean War, we know that at least one Walsingham volunteer was involved because his cemetery gravestone records his death on board ship en route to Turkey.[6] And with the Boer War (1899-1902) volunteers left as a party in February 1900 and, as they assembled at

Male Occupations 1841-1891

YEAR	MALE POPULATION	MALE WORKERS	FARMING inc. Ag. Labs.	BUILDING TRADES	LEATHER TRADES inc. Shoemaking	DISTRIBUTION TRADES	SERVICE TRADES	PUBLIC OFFICIALS
1841	510	277	97	35	37	52	15	6
1851	544	336	124	37	35	79	12	8
1861	484	318	142	34	23	55	20	10
1871	451	298	121	37	26	48	19	6
1881	460	270	101	37	15	51	24	9
1891	439	239	104	28	9	66	27	11

Source: Walsingham Enumerators' Schedules 1841 - 1891; Norfolk Records Office)

Fakenham railway station, two little girls from Walsingham presented the volunteers with gifts purchased as a result of the collection they had organised.[7]

In 1872 the coming of a farm-workers Union to Norfolk created quite a stir. A branch of the Norfolk (later National) Agricultural Labourers' Union was established in Walsingham in that year and the Union's founder and president, Joseph Arch, came to Walsingham several times, attracting substantial gatherings of workers, often in their hundreds. The Union, which included many older and staid labourers, had close identification with the Primitive Methodists and its leaders were often preachers and officials of the Ranters, as Primitive Methodists were called. Union meetings are known to have been held in the Primitives' Chapel, starting with prayers and hymns. Since many labourers were illiterate, Union songs with rousing choruses were sung to familiar hymn tunes. The Union sought better conditions for farmworkers, better wages, and shorter hours and it also opposed Hiring and Statute Fairs, such as the one held annually in Walsingham. The Union encouraged emigration and even had its own emigration officer in the village. But in 1874, the farmers retaliated, organised lock-outs, brought in black-leg labour, etc. which nearly destroyed the Union. Although the Walsingham District was one of the most active and was prominent in the 1890 revival, the times were not propitious and the Union finally ceased in 1895.

Nationally, in the Victorian years, nearly 64% of all female workers were domestic servants, closely matched by the Walsingham figure of nearly 66%. In 1851 the youngest female servant in Walsingham was aged 10 and that Census shows that between ages 10-19, a third of all females are servants, rising to nearly 60% between ages 20-29. With so few in-village work

Female Occupations 1841 - 1891

YEAR	FEMALE POPULATION	FEMALE WORKERS	DOMESTIC SERVANTS	SERVANTS AS % OF FEMALE WORKFORCE	DISTRIBUTION TRADES
1841	581	102	81	79%	14
1851	597	162	96	59%	51
1861	566	158	98	62%	37
1871	565	155	99	64%	41
1881	550	146	98	67%	32
1891	485	136	87	64%	38

(Source: Walsingham Enumerators' Schedules 1841-1891; Norfolk Records Office.)

opportunities some girls would be kept at home to look after the family in the hope of a 'good' employment vacancy arising. The only other major work opportunities for most girls centred around dress-making and, as the century wore on, shop work.

Middle class professionals, shop proprietors and craft work employers might be able to make provision for family members within their firms. The 1871 Census for Norfolk revealed that although more than 5,000 boys aged 5 to 14 were engaged in agriculture, only 150 were craft apprentices. Victoria's later years did open up some areas of opportunity and for Walsingham the chief one related to the advent of the railway in 1857 offering both manual and clerical work.

It might seem a digression to focus just for a moment on boot and shoe craftworkers but the demise of this occupation is symptomatic of the decline of 19th century Walsingham. In 1851, shoemaking by hand[8] was still one of the ten largest occupational groups in the country, yet by the end of the century its decline as a craft skill was almost complete. The figures for Walsingham show the change from 33 all male workers in 1841, to a height in 1851 of 35 workers, including four females, down to 22 in 1871, 11 workers in 1881[9] and by 1896[10] only one person in Kelly's Directory is described solely as a bootmaker, although machine-made footwear could be bought from a general dealer who doubled as postmaster and insurance agent.

Health and Medicine. In Victoria's reign doctors remained expensive, typically charging a guinea to be present at a childbirth whereas the village midwife's charge was 2s 6d. The commonest ailment was general debility, probably exacerbated by overcrowded housing, which also encouraged the spread of infections. We have Walsingham examples of 14 people living in a two roomed cottage and even at the end of the century, children sleeping head to toe in the same bed in a Cokers Hill dwelling. A particular example is of an agricultural labourer, his wife (a field-woman, i.e. working in the fields), six children all under 12. The eldest, a girl was employed as a servant girl, or skivvy. The next oldest, her 10 year old brother, worked in the fields from 6 a.m. to 8 p.m. for a few coppers a day, plus the man's widowed mother and his wife's widower father, both described as paupers and finally, to ensure sufficient income, two male lodgers. It is not clear whether these 12 people lived in a two roomed cottage or simply one with just two bedrooms, but since one of those rooms would be no more than 7 feet by 8 feet, the degree of overcrowding, with its physical and moral hazards, can barely by imagined.[11]

Housing and Occupancy in Walsingham 1841-1891

The absence of running water, for example, in the village school, the prevalence of lice and nits in the hair and the smell of unwashed children at school (for all of which we have Walsingham examples) give an idea of the

	1841	1851	1861	1871	1881	1891
Total inhabited houses	238	262	259	252	226	231
Houses uninhabited or being built	9	9	16 (NB Cokers Hill)	5	20	19
Total population	1091	1141	1050	1016	1010	924
Average occupancy (persons per house)	4.5	4.3	4.0	4.0	4.4	4.0
More than 6 persons per house	76	77	56	59	70	56
(including) 8 or more per house	29	26	21	21	29	21
1 or 2 persons per house (including servant as appropriate)	58	68	68	72	50	78

(Source: Walsingham Enumerators' Schedules 1841-1891; Norfolk Records Office.)

normal situation. Illegitimacy was high in Norfolk, confirmed for Walsingham by the Union Workhouse birth register and the Walsingham Census details.

By the later 19th century, a conscientious labourer could join a Friendly or Benefit Society. Then, by paying a small subscription, he could ensure some income in the event of sickness or to cover funeral expenses. In Walsingham, the principal Friendly Society was the Loyal Lee Warner Lodge of the Manchester Unity of Oddfellows. Founded in the village in 1857, it had 80 male members in 1870. A benefit subscription table for 1897 shows that a 24 year old labourer paying 2½d a week could receive 7s. a week for 12 months in the event of sickness or accident, whilst for 2s 9d. a year there would be death cover of £7 for himself and £3 10s. for his wife's death. As a Friendly Society it had monthly meetings at the Bull with a splendid annual Anniversary Celebration, including a Parade to the Parish Church, behind a band, then on to Houghton, back to the Abbey and finally a village dinner with the Chair taken by the Squire. Another Walsingham Benefit organisation was the Robin Hood Burial Society, which paid out £10 on the death of a member and in 1864 had 392 members. But a labourer too poor to subscribe for Society benefits might hope for some help from village charities, such as the payment at Christmas of 5s. and coal to widows and pensioners or the occasional hand-out of a village altruist such as Dr. Hudson who gave 36 widows half a crown each.

In 1838 when the Walsingham Union Workhouse was erected some 2½ miles away just outside Thursford, the regime in new workhouses, based on the so-called principle of least eligibility, was severe and disciplined. Labourers seeking work together with their families, might trek from one workhouse to another. On arrival they were subjected to a compulsory bath, deloused and, as recompense for food supplied to a strict schedule, tasks were imposed. Men were segregated from women, children from their parents.

The topic of **law and order** had particular relevance for Walsingham where the Quarter Sessions had been held from 1778 and by Victoria's accession the prestige for the village which this involved was firmly established. Whilst the Shire Hall housed these Sessions, the Petty Sessions took place monthly in the Black Lion and although the latter dealt only with so-called petty or minor crimes, penalties could still involve up to six months in the Bridewell and even a private whipping. The third village legal element in 1837 was the Bridewell, or House of Correction, built in 1787 and later extended to house more than 50 prisoners, often a few females, the majority of males being agricultural labourers. But in 1861 the position for Walsingham changed. The Quarter Sessions were transferred elsewhere allowing the less important Petty Sessions to move from the Black Lion to the Shire Hall and in the same year the Bridewell also closed, part of the premises then being utilised as a police station.

The growth of temperance. Throughout Victoria's reign there were always six or seven Inns, public houses or beer shops in Walsingham and up to 20% of the labourer's income might be spent in a pub. Such extravagance represented an alternative to the squalid over-crowded, bleak dwelling technically called home. Drunkenness was, at first, prevalent, with peaks in the 1840s and 1870s, but eventually Opening Hours were curtailed, still leaving it possible to obtain a drink between 5 a.m. and half past midnight.

Against this background the temperance movements were established during the 1830s. Particularly associated with Methodism, their virtues were also espoused by farmers and employers. The Salvation Army in Walsingham from 1885, called on drinkers to sign the pledge. Several other temperance related organisations were active, such as the Temperance Working Men's Mutual Improvement Society, with a branch in Wells. Walsingham itself saw the foundation of the Abbeygate Coffee House, probably in 1866, with support from the Earl of Leicester and which, by 1882 is described as the Abbeygate Temperance Hotel and Restaurant and later incorporated a Club Reading Room and Institute.

On the basis that literacy may be defined as the ability to sign one's name a brief look at **literacy and education**. An analysis of 309 marriages recorded in the Walsingham Marriage Registers for 1837-1900 shows 107 involved agricultural labourers and of these 87 were illiterate and in 88 cases their wives were illiterate. The Registers reveal a steady decline from 68% illiteracy in the late 1830s to 2% in the 1890s, with an average close to the national figure of 20% among agricultural labourers in 1871.

However, considering that the village contained a Grammar School, opened again in 1841 after being closed for at least 20 years, and which had about 30 pupils in 1875, and also the construction of the National or Church of England school in 1841/42, giving places for 180 boys and girls and 80 infants, we might consider it disappointing that village literacy was not better than average. Formal schooling was not the only variety. Sunday schools from 1780 taught children to read, write and say the catechism, but with the improvements in secular education, Sunday schools then specialised in religious education.

Religious denominations in Victorian Walsingham. At the beginning of the 19th century, only two denominations had Walsingham Meeting places, i.e. the Anglicans and the Wesleyan Methodists. In 1835, the Independents or Congregationalists, established a presence in the village, followed by the erection of their small chapel in 1840, but largely they viewed Walsingham as a missionary territory and few ministers stayed long. Their chapel was sold to the Unattached Methodists after 1868.

The original Wesleyan congregation with its chapel and wide variety of organisations continued throughout the entire century, although periodic financial difficulties required the Minister to forego some of his income. The building of its own Sunday school, the strength of its Class Meetings and its importance in the circuit, suggest a largely untroubled existence, but in 1849 breakaway or Unattached Methodists, objecting to the Wesleyans' priestly-like administration, wanted a body organised from the bottom up and not from the top down. By 1851 (see Religious Census) some 60 breakaway Methodists appear to have ceased worshipping in the Wesleyan chapel and had started to meet elsewhere. Not until 1868, when they purchased the ex-Congregationalists chapel do they seem to have their own meeting place but after 1875 we cannot trace any further reference to their village existence.

Another strand of Methodism, the Primitives or Ranters, established a Fakenham Circuit from 1825 and had become sufficiently numerous in Walsingham by 1848/49 as to erect their own chapel. Whereas Wesleyans appealed more to small shopkeepers, small farmers and skilled agricultural labourers, Ranters particularly attracted ordinary agricultural labourers, especially those less than fully employed and those with larger families. Wesleyans had regular Ministers and an on-going organisational framework, but the Ranters relied on leaders from within their own ranks, building up their ooown local organisation and appealing to the more disadvantaged. In hard times Methodists sought to help their own Brethren and certainly assisted those who chose to migrate to other areas, such as in pursuit of employment. The 1870s and 1880s witnessed strong associations with the Agricultural Labourers Union, who even held meetings in the Primitive Methodists' Chapel and whose officers were Methodist Preachers and leaders.

The Salvation Army were established in their barracks in Knight Street from 1885 until 1909. We also have a press report from the 1875 Norfolk News that at the time of Walsingham annual fair a party of Revivalists from London went about the village, holding open-air meetings and singing Sankey and Moody hymns. In 1897 we have the first public Roman Catholic pilgrimage to Walsingham for over 350 years, even if the only identified Catholic, and that in 1904, was a nurse at the Workhouse.

The Church of England was long established, well-endowed and closely supported by the Lee Warners. The Anglican Church administered the National School, superintended the charities and was supported by the principal families, the gentry and those who wished to be seen attending the

National Religious Census 1851 (carried out on March 30th, Mid-Lent Sunday)

Returns for Little Walsingham

DENOMINATION	MAXIMUM ATTENDANCE ANY ONE SERVICE	SUNDAY SCHOOL SCHOL-ARS	TOTAL SITTINGS	of which FREE SITTINGS	MEETING PLACE AND EXCLUSIVITY (E)
Church of England	202	95	498	128	Church (E) Consecrated pre 1800
Wesleyan Methodists	116	17	440	220	Chapel (E) Erected pre 1800
Primitive Methodists	172	73	226	50	Chapel (E) Erected 1848
Wesleyan Union	64	n/a	80	80 (and 50 standing)	Non-exclusive use of Meeting Place
Independents (i.e. Congregationalists)	69	16	200		Chapel (E) From 1840
[Not Listed: Bridewell]					Chapel (E)
	623	= Total nominal maximum attendance			

Nationally, between 47% and 54% of population aged 10 and over were at Church or Chapel on that Sunday. Little Walsingham total of 623 (but subject to caveats) out of total all age population of 1141 shows a higher than national average, i.e. approximately 55% without excluding children under 10 years.

National proportions: Anglicans: Nonconformists approx. 50:50

Walsingham proportions: Anglicans: Nonconformists approx. 33:67

Parish Church. Interesting details show that in 1882 the average Sunday collection was 9s 10½d., with 25 communicants, but in that year a remarkable 800 attended Harvest Festival Evensong in the parish church. The arrival of Rev. George Woodward as incumbent in 1882 (he is the famous author of Ding Dong Merrily on High and This Joyful Eastertide), introduced a different dimension in church life. He organised choirboys at Easter to sing carols as they processed around the village and by 1887 had introduced both daily communion and probably such daily services as choral evensong.

Finally we will look at **Travel**. A traveller visiting Walsingham in 1837 would travel over roads maintained by turnpike monies whichever way he came because at least three turnpike Tollhouses 'guarded' the routes into the village requiring the payment of toll monies before users proceeded further.

In 1837 regular horse-drawn coach and carrier services connected Walsingham with Wells, Fakenham and Norwich and thereafter to London. Such services, at least three times per week, stopped at the Black Lion for passengers to board or alight. Travelling in such a way took about one and a quarter hours from Wells to Fakenham, or from Wells to London 12 hours at an average speed of ten miles per hour and a cost of 6d. per mile. When railways began operations in Norfolk in the 1840s it was possible to take a coach from Walsingham to Brandon to connect with the Norwich and London trains. Even until the end of the century, horse-drawn wagons and vans continued regular services from the Bull, the King's Head and the Black Lion.

No consideration of Victorian Walsingham would be complete without a consideration of **the coming of the railway** and its consequences. The Fakenham to Wells line, stopping en-route at Walsingham and Wighton, finally opened on 1st December 1857, an occasion of great excitement, a public holiday in Walsingham with banners, bands and crowds and at night celebrations, including a bonfire in Friday Market. The line was actually an extension of the Wymondham to Fakenham railway and had cost more than £70,000 to build, of which Lord Leicester put up £11,000. Part of the relatively heavy cost was due to construction difficulties at Barsham, which required a massive wooden viaduct and the building of a tunnel nearly a quarter of a mile long.

Eventually the Fakenham to Wells railway settled down as a feeder line with five services a day and it is said sometimes no more then five people were waiting to board a train at any one station. Indeed, by the 1890s when the Barsham tunnel was converted to a cutting and the soil thereof used to create an embankment in place of the unsatisfactory viaduct, it could be doubted whether the line on its own was strictly viable.

Even a small railway station such as Walsingham became for a time the new focus of village interest, combining the sights and sounds of steam engines, evidence of change and new inventions and even providing an occasional view of important people. A new Inn opened opposite the railway station in the 1860s and pragmatic village entrepreneurs taking advantage of the new facilities developed coal and coke rounds, acted as carriers of goods to and from the railway yard and provided connections for passengers to and from their homes. The railway offered a more convenient and cheaper way of moving agricultural produce and it even provided a facility for moving to Norwich Castle Jail those so sentenced at the Magistrates' Court.

But the railways aggravated the demise of local industries, quickening for example the decline of specialist furniture manufacturers and of the Walsingham boot and shoe trade. Cheaper, mass-produced products were brought in, of greater variety and quality. Cheaper foodstuffs eventually helped improve the standard of living of agricultural labourers in regular employment, but contributed to the undermining of arable farming from the 1870s, with its consequences for landowners, farmers and those farm workers relying on casual employment. Stage-coaches were made redundant, resulting in a plethora of businesses which lost trade such as the proprietors of coaching inns and their numerous employees, the substantial craft trade in making and repairing coaches, and those who supplied and provided horses. One could make a case for describing the railway as the agent of exciting change, but in conjunction with other developments such as the opening of the Fakenham cattle market in 1857 we argue that the railway was, in reality, for Walsingham the harbinger of decline, resulting in lost employment opportunities, the complete demise of craft industries, the disappearance of Walsingham's own market and producing, by the end of the century a continuously declining community, with few occupations other than those concerned with arable farming.

In conclusion, we will try and condense all these varying aspects of Victorian life in Walsingham on to a single canvas and in a few broad brush strokes. When we start, in 1837, Walsingham was a centre of relative importance, with a wealthy land-owning Squire, numerous gentry and a substantial arable farming community and also noted for its craft-based enterprises such as making specialist regional furniture and, of course, its boot and shoe trade, the second most important source of employment in the village. It was the focus of local justice administration with both Quarter and Petty Sessions held on a regular basis, plus a long-established Bridewell. It was served regularly by coach and wagon but was sufficiently self-contained that for many of its inhabitants the world was Walsingham and Walsingham was the world. Thus most Walsingham citizens felt no desire to travel; they lacked curiosity and would regard any journey of more than a few miles as bringing them to the edge of the known world. When the Walsingham Union Workhouse opened in Thursford in 1838 it might have been seen as an omen of change to come, but would have been dismissed as too far away for it to have any substantial effect.

This attitude of laissez-faire might have been expected to continue into the 1840s. Railway mania elsewhere would still have left the village relatively insulated from impending change. Indeed, the most significant events in that decade were very local: the re-opening of the Grammar School and the building of the National School, even if many children failed to attend as a result of family poverty. But in a community as tightly-knit as Walsingham it was the changes in the Methodist church which would have produced the strongest feelings. Firstly, there was the opening of the Primitive Methodist Chapel as evidence of the rapid growth of its separate congregation, but with its particular appeal to the least privileged, including the under-employed and the unemployed. Secondly came the breakaway within the Wesleyan congregation itself, producing a new 'floating' body without its own separate meeting place, probably some 60 strong and resulting, doubtless, in bitter feelings.

In its way the 1850s marked the fulcrum, the highspot of Victorian Walsingham. Craft trades such as boot and shoe manufacture was still expanding and during the decade the establishment of the Oddfellows in the village gave a safety net against disaster for all those who could afford its modest subscriptions. But head and shoulders above all other happenings in the 1850s was the coming of the railway, seemingly an occasion of rejoicing, with the prospects of a new and better future. Yet a knowing crystal-gazer might have said it would be better if the line had never come since, in the end, it contributed more to the village's decline than to its potential for growth.

Evidence of this decline soon came when, in the 1860s, the village ceased to house the Quarter Sessions and lost, also, the Bridewell. The cattle market opening in Fakenham in 1857 brought about the final disappearance of Walsingham's own livestock market. The village and its immediate locality was the epi-centre for the outbreak of Scarlet Fever in 1864, producing a substantial rise in village death, mostly amongst children. As the years progressed, the outlook for an arable-farming based community deteriorated and the 1870s saw the beginning of the Great Depression which lasted for more than 20 years. Almost without exception the 1870s were a time of bad or very bad weather, contributing to the increasingly depressed state of arable farming. These years saw the rise of the National Agricultural Labourers' Union, with particular strength in Walsingham, and which saw village meetings packed with several hundred farmworkers. In retaliation, farmers organised a labour lock-out and in combination with the substantial membership losses resulting from Union-encouraged emigration, the effectiveness of this protest body declined.

The 1880s saw a range of national as well as local happenings. Rural males finally received the vote in 1884, and some would hold that of greatest significance was the initiation of compulsory school attendance, initially for ages 5 to 10, but opposed by some parents and at first subject to considerable truancy. Within the village, the struggle for temperance and against drunkenness witnessed the coming into operation of the Abbeygate Coffee House, Temperance Hotel and workers' Reading Rooms. By now the decline and ultimate defeat of the craft-based occupations was becoming rampant. At the parish church, meanwhile, Parson Woodward introduced and encouraged church choral singing at about the same time as the Salvation Army was establishing itself and its band in the village.

So to the 1890s and up to Victoria's death in 1901. At this time Walsingham was described as small and unimportant, chiefly composed of one long narrow street with a little square. Internationally it was the time of the South African or Boer Wars, when a flood of young men from the countryside were attracted to the army by the prospect of adventure and the glamour of a smart uniform. But had they known that one in six of Norfolk volunteers would die, chiefly from fever or disease, they might have been less enthusiastic. School attendance was now compulsory to age 12. With cheaper food and other consumable costs and when wages finally rose to 15s. a week, agricultural labourers in regular employment felt better off.

Yet to the end of our period Walsingham's decline continued unabated, whether we consider population figures now down to their lowest level, or the virtual disappearance of craft trades. The absence of alternative employment locally for restless youngsters led to a continual haemorrhaging of such young people in their search for work, leading to an unbalanced ageing population, predictably depicted in the archetypal caricature of the rural labourer as ill-shod, ill-clothed, near-illiterate, under-nourished and under-employed. It was against this background that the first Catholic pilgrimage for 350 years came to the village, the precursor of greater change in the community than had been caused by the coming of the railway and with hindsight, again marking an eventual turning point in the on-going history of Walsingham.

REFERENCES

1. R. J. Evans, In defence of History, Granta (1997).
2. F. Crouzet, trans. by A. S. Forster, The Victorian Economy, London, Methuen (1982).
3. Burial Registers held at Norfolk Records Office.
4. F. Crouzet, op. cit.
5. A. Digby, Pauper Palaces, London, Routledge & Kegan Paul (1978)
6. St. Mary's, Walsingham, churchyard: gravestone for F. Purdy, who died on his passage to Turkey.
7. Norwich Mercury, 3 February 1900.
8. June Swann, Shoemaking, Princes Risborough, Shire. (1986).
9. Details from Walsingham Enumerators' Schedules 1841-1881 (Norfolk Records Office)
10. Kelly's 1896 Norfolk Directory.
11. Walsingham Enumerators' Schedule 1861.

THE DEVELOPMENT OF MODERN DAY PILGRIMAGE

by Canon Peter G Cobb

The restoration of pilgrimage to Walsingham amongst Roman Catholics seems to be due mainly to the labours of Father George Wrigglesworth, Missionary Rector of King's Lynn, and Father Philip Fletcher, the co-founder and Master of the Guild of Our Lady of Ransom. Even after Catholic Emancipation and the Second Spring there was no very public cultus of Our Lady. Devotion to her was solid but quiet. Churches did not necessarily have a statue of her and outdoor processions were not a feature of Marian devotion. The memory of pilgrimage to Walsingham had grown very faint. Father Bridgett's book *Our Lady's Dowry*, published in 1875, has only a few pages on Walsingham, although this was more than rectified by Edmund Waterton's great work *Pietas Mariana Britannica* published four years later. When Father Wrigglesworth and Father Fletcher built the Shrine Chapel of the Holy House of Nazareth in the new Church of the Annunciation in King's Lynn in 1897, they clearly intended to revive pilgrimage in honour of Our Lady of Walsingham and saw the Shrine at Lynn as only an interim measure. One of the purposes of the Guild of Ransom was "to revive old Catholic customs in England such as processions of Our Lady and pilgrimages".[1] Father Fletcher certainly hoped that there would be a return to Walsingham. He wrote to a friend:

> I do not think there would be difficulty in restoring the shrine to Walsingham eventually ... The reason why King's Lynn was chosen some years ago was that there was a resident priest and congregation there, who could keep up the devotion and guard the shrine...Nothing of this kind was possible at Walsingham when Father Wrigglesworth and I began the restoration...We must keep to King's Lynn for the present but may hope and pray to see Walsingham restored when a mission can be established there.[2]

It is significant that on 20th August 1897, the day after the statue of Our Lady of Walsingham had been solemnly received and installed in the new shrine in Lynn, a party of some 40 or 50 people travelled by train from Lynn to Walsingham and processed from the station, led by a crucifix with burning tapers on either side of it, and singing as they went, to the recently restored Slipper Chapel, where there was a short service, after which they went to lunch at the Black Lion.[3] Nevertheless the official centre of devotion to Our Lady of Walsingham, established on the authority of the Pope himself, was the Shrine in King's Lynn. There, daily devotions were held and to it an annual pilgrimage, led by the Guild of Our Lady of Ransom, went every year until the Slipper Chapel became the National Shrine of Our Lady of Walsingham in 1934, and indeed in subsequent years.[4]

The Slipper Chapel was cared for, but the Bishop of Northampton, in whose jurisdiction it then lay, would not allow mass to be celebrated there. Individuals undoubtedly visited the Chapel as pilgrims and said their prayers, but there were no organised pilgrimages to it.[5] All that changed in 1934 when it was declared the National Shrine of Our Lady of Walsingham. A new statue of Our Lady, modelled on the seal of the medieval priory in Walsingham, like that set up by Father Alfred Hope Patten in the Anglican parish church in Walsingham 12 years earlier, was enthroned in the Slipper Chapel by Bishop Youens on 16th August and, on 19th August, Cardinal Bourne, accompanied by eight other bishops, led a huge pilgrimage to Walsingham. The numbers have been variously estimated as 10,000, 12,000, even 19,000.[6]

In July 1935, a special train brought the first Westminster Cathedral pilgrimage which met up with the first walking pilgrimage, a party of men and women who had walked from London, following as far as possible the ancient pilgrims' way. The first pilgrimage party which stayed overnight was a coachload of 'old girls' from the Roehampton Sacred Heart School, who came to keep the Annunciation in 1936. Also in 1936, there began a series of pilgrimages made up of children who came to pray for their schools. In 1938, the 400th anniversary of the destruction of the medieval shrine, there was another huge pilgrimage, led this time by Cardinal Hinsley, the National Pilgrimage of Catholic Youth. About 10,000 young people took part, according to *The Times*. It culminated in a moving scene when the Cardinal laid a wreath of lilies on the site of the original Holy House in the Abbey grounds.[7]

The increasing number of pilgrims required more accommodation. In 1936 a pilgrims' hostel was opened in Friday Market[8] and two years later an additional Chapel of the Holy Ghost was built next to the Slipper Chapel. It has been estimated that in 1938 a total of 50,000 Roman Catholics made the pilgrimage to Walsingham.[9]

The revival of pilgrimage to Walsingham amongst Anglicans has a very different background. It must be seen in the context of the Romantic Movement which popularised and romanticised the Middle Ages. This led to an antiquarian interest in surviving medieval buildings, cathedrals and churches, and in the remains of the dispoiled religious homes. Excavations were made in their ruins, such as that by James Lee Warner at Walsingham Priory in the early 1850s.[10] It also led to an exploration of medieval spiritual life. There was a widespread interest in the idea of pilgrimage in mainstream Anglicanism. From 1877 a series of books on the Pilgrim's Way to Canterbury appeared[11] which resulted in various cathedrals making a conscious effort to promote themselves as centres of pilgrimage. Dean Bennett of Chester was particularly active in this. He even reintroduced pilgrim badges of St. Werburgh's shrine in 1925. George Bell, then Dean of Canterbury, got representatives of the parishes to make a diocesan pilgrimage to the cathedral in 1920. The following year was the 1300th anniversary of the founding of York Minster and 95 parishes were persuaded to make separate pilgrimages there. In 1934, in the Great Depression there were nationwide pilgrimages to cathedrals to pray for the unemployed. Even the King and Queen went to Westminster Abbey on such a pilgrimage and wore pilgrim badges.[12]

The pilgrimage to Walsingham derives more directly, however, from the Catholic Revival in the 19th century Church of England, the Oxford Movement and its subsequent phases, the Ritualist and Anglo Catholic movements. This owed something to the Romantic Movement but was more a theological and spiritual renewal. It was, however, slow to develop any cultus of Our Lady. Towards the end of the century, some of the more 'extreme' societies were recommending Marian devotions and the use of the rosary. It was really only in the first quarter of this century, however, that Marian devotion in the Church of England really developed. In about 1904 the League of Our Lady was founded under the presidency of Lord Halifax. In 1931 it amalgamated with the Confraternity of Our Lady, which was started in Madras in 1880 and had itself united in 1920 with the Union of the Holy Rosary, founded in 1886, to form the Society of Mary.[13] The League was to play a vital role in the revival of pilgrimage to Walsingham as Father Hope Patten himself acknowledged.[14] Another organisation which played an important part in the early days was the papalist Catholic League, founded in 1913.[15]

Support for the revival of pilgrimage, then, came from only one section, one party as some would express it, of the Church of England. The rest, the majority, were either indifferent or hostile. Even The Church Times was critical. Moreover, there was no official sanction, let alone support for it, but rather the opposite. Father Hope Patten skilfully manoeuvred the Bishop of Norwich, Bertram Pollock, into agreeing to the shrine being moved from the parish church into a chapel on private property but the Bishop would never agree to licensing the shrine for the celebration of the Eucharist.[16] Some bishops expressed open hostility. Henley Henson, the Bishop of Durham, visited Walsingham in 1926 and published an article in *The Evening Standard* ridiculing the shrine and claiming that the revival of pilgrimage was part of the general [Anglo-Catholic] policy of "undoing the Reformation".[17]

The revival of pilgrimage to the shrine in the parish church began, consequently, in a very small way. The first pilgrimage was planned by the League of Our Lady for 24th/26th October 1922. Arrangements were made to accommodate 40 pilgrims. In the event only three arrived, but, by a stroke of genius Hope Patten persuaded the villagers to make the pilgrimage themselves.[18] The pilgrims were Father Gordon Hibbs and two sisters, Constance and Emma Bailey. The next pilgrimage, the following May, was better organised. Over 40 pilgrims came, about half of them from London.[19] After that the League tried to arrange two pilgrimages a year, one in May and the other in August. In the summer of 1927 the first pilgrimage organised by the Catholic League came, led by Father Fynes-Clinton, and that too became an annual fixture.[20] The shrine's own organisation, the Society of Our Lady of Walsingham founded in 1925, also organised an annual pilgrimage. Most of

Shrine of Our Lady of Walsingham in St. Mary's Parish Church.

these early pilgrimages were mid-week because Wednesday was the only day that the grounds of the Abbey were open and an integral part of the programme, besides receiving the sacraments and doing the Stations of the Cross, was visiting the site of the original Holy House and drinking water from the wells there. A visit was also made to the Slipper Chapel for prayers and devotions. Pilgrims were originally accommodated in the homes of parishioners in the village, but in 1926 a permanent hospice was established, the Hospice of Our Lady Star of the Sea[21] and a refectory made out of a former barn. A Pilgrims' Manual was produced in 1928 and by then a pilgrims' badge had been struck.

The building of the Holy House and its covering chapel and the translation of the statue to it from the parish church on 15th October 1931 altered the character of the pilgrimage. The attendant publicity attracted more people; the focus of the pilgrimage moved to the new Shrine and regular pilgrimages were organised at the weekend. This meant that pilgrims could no longer visit the Abbey grounds but Hope Patten believed that this was no longer necessary as he was convinced that the ancient remains discovered on the site of the new shrine were those of the original medieval shrine. During the first year after the opening, he calculated that there were 7,080 pilgrims excluding those who came in July when no records were kept; in 1935 12,700 passed through the Shrine; and in 1936 15,000.[22]

Tranlation of the Statue of Our Lady of Walsingham to the new Anglican Shrine.

The increased numbers led to the extension of the shrine in 1938 to provide for a total of 15 Altars. On 6th June, the day of the blessing of the extension, 6,000 are said to have passed through the Holy House.[23] The following Whit Monday was kept as the anniversary of the completion of the shrine by what came to be regarded by Anglicans as the first National Pilgrimage, now an annual event on the Spring Bank Holiday. It was the largest pilgrimage to date of about 12,000 people.[24] Altogether, in the last year before the war, there were said to have been 30,900 pilgrims and visitors to the shrine.[25]

For most of the war Walsingham was within a prohibited area. Organised pilgrimages were not allowed. Father Hope Patten encouraged Anglicans to make a spiritual pilgrimage at the shrines to Our Lady of Walsingham which were set up in various parish churches throughout the country. From time to time, however, the ban was lifted. The Catholic League, for example, made a pilgrimage in the winter of 1943.[26] There were many military bases in East Anglia, and members of the allied forces, and indeed a few prisoners of war, visited both shrines. Just after the war, on 17th May 1945, Roman Catholic members of the American forces came to Walsingham for a High Mass celebrated in the presence of the Bishop of Northampton on the site of the high altar in the ruins of the priory, the first since the revival of pilgrimage and indeed since the reformation.[27]

Pilgrimages were rather slow to start again after the war. Father Hope Patten complained there was not much enthusiasm for a pilgrimage of thanksgiving.[28] In 1948, however, the Roman Catholics organised a huge pilgrimage of Prayer and Penance for Peace, similar to one to Vézélay in France the previous year. Fourteen groups of men carried oak crosses, nine foot in height, from different parts of the country to Walsingham where the Union of Catholic Mothers were also making their third annual pilgrimage. Over 12,000 took part altogether.[29]

From then on, the number of pilgrims to Walsingham has steadily increased, in spite of the closure of the railway in 1964. There are some fairly obvious reasons for this. In the Roman Catholic Church there was a great interest in Mariology in the post-war years leading up to the promulgation of the dogma of the Assumption of Our Lady in 1950. 1954 was a Marian year and some 20,000 people were drawn to Walsingham on The Feast of the Assumption when Archbishop O'Hara, the Apostolic Delegate, crowned a new statue of Our Lady of Walsingham.[30] The Anglican Shrine gradually became more acceptable to the Church of England as a whole. In 1965 the Bishop of Southwark, Mervyn Stockwood, preached at the National Pilgrimage, the first English diocesan bishop to do so. Seven years later, the Bishop of Norwich himself graciously accepted a similar invitation and in 1980 the Archbishop of Canterbury came. Another sign of the acceptance of the Shrine by the wider church was that in 1983 the then Master of the College of Guardians, David Hope, was made Bishop of Wakefield. He was later translated to London and then became Archbishop of York.

It is difficult to measure the increase in the number of pilgrims for the lack of statistics but a few facts give an impression. At the Anglican Shrine in 1948, 21 parish pilgrimages booked in; this year (1998) there are 360. *Our Lady's Mirror* reported that about 1,000 took part in the National Pilgrimage on Whit Monday in 1950, and again in 1951 and 1953. In 1959, in expectation of larger numbers to celebrate the centenary of the Church Union, the mass was celebrated in the Abbey grounds for the first time, as it has been in most subsequent years. There seem to be no comparable figures for the Roman Catholic Shrine. Claude Fisher estimated that in 1980, when Cardinal Hume led a Westminster Diocesan Pilgrimage to the Roman Catholic Shrine on 11th May and Archbishop Robert Runcie led the Anglican National Pilgrimage a fortnight later, 10,000 Roman Catholics and 15,000 Anglicans took part.[31] In 1996 the English Tourist Board calculated that there were 250,000 pilgrims and visitors to Walsingham but this is probably an over-estimate.

The increasing number of pilgrims is reflected in the additions to the shrine churches and extra provision of accommodation for pilgrims to stay. The Anglican Shrine Church was widened by a north cloister (aisle) added in 1964, in memory of Father Hope Patten, and a south cloister added in 1972 to commemorate the jubilee of the setting up of the shrine in the Parish church.[32] The first additional pilgrim accommodation was built in 1956 when the gate house and extra rooms were built next to the Hospice of Our Lady Star of the Sea.[33] Then in 1985 St. Joseph's Wing was added to provide special accommodation for the disabled[34] and finally in 1990 Richeldis House was opened.[35] The present refectory was built as a temporary measure, in 1969[36] and there are plans to replace it by the Millenium. At the Roman Catholic Shrine the eirenically named Chapel of Reconciliation was added in 1982, partly in the hope that Pope John Paul would come to Walsingham on his visit to England in that year.[37] Five years later a further building, including a shop and cafe was added 'to cope with the growing volume of pilgrims'.[38] The provision of accommodation and eating facilities for the Roman Catholic pilgrims is a more complicated story. According to Claude Fisher, Aelred House, which was the first building in Walsingham to be owned by Catholics (since 1934), became a pilgrim hostel in 1948 and was replaced in the 1970s by the former Oddfellows Hall (now the Parish Hall), which was converted into a Pilgrims' Refectory. This in turn was later exchanged for the old National School. At different times other buildings were used such as the former King's Head, (now Guisborough House). The Roman Catholic pilgrimage accommodation is now consolidated on one site, Elmham House, the former Grammar School, which has recently been extended.[39]

Pilgrimage to Walsingham has grown and one hopes will continue to grow. It has also become ecumenical. The annual Student Cross pilgrimage in Holy Week which began in 1948, the year of the great Pilgrimage of Prayer and Penance for Peace, became officially ecumenical in 1972.[40] The first general ecumenical pilgrimage took place in 1971;[41] and the first inter-diocesan pilgrimage, the Sussex Anglican-Roman Catholic Pilgrimage, in 1981, when the Anglican Bishop of Chichester and the Roman Catholic Bishop of Arundel and Brighton themselves led their dioceses to Walsingham.[42]

In 1982, when the statue of Our Lady of Walsingham was taken up to London to the Pope's Mass at Wembley, the Anglican Administrator was graciously invited to carry it into the stadium with the Director of the National Shrine.[43]

The search for the unity of the church is bound up with the revival of pilgrimage to Walsingham. The yearning for re-union, especially union with Rome, lies at the heart of the Catholic Revival in the Church of England.[44] Lord Halifax, the inspirer with the Abbé Portal of the dialogue between Anglicans and Catholics in the 1890s, and of the Malines Conversations in the 1920s, was responsible also for the founding of the League of Our Lady. The Catholic League, led by Father Fynes-Clinton, was specifically committed to reunion between the Church of England and the Roman Catholic Church, and was instrumental in organising the Week of Prayer for Christian Unity in England. It was these two societies which pioneered pilgrimage to Walsingham amongst Anglicans and Lord Halifax and Father Fynes-Clinton were two of the original guardians of the Holy House in 1931. It is significant too that many of those who were responsible for reviving the pilgrimage to Walsingham amongst Roman Catholics - Father Philip Fletcher, Charlotte Boyd, Father Bruno Scott James and Claude Fisher - were all former Anglicans, formed in that tradition, though they took the way of individual submission.

There was some opposition to Anglicans visiting the Slipper Chapel in the early days, although in fact on one occasion at least, when Anglicans had been excluded and Hope Patten complained, he received a gracious apology from the authorities.[45] Ironically the prayers which the Anglicans were to say outside the Chapel according to the Pilgrims' Manual of 1928 were for "the reunion of these provinces [York and Canterbury] and the whole of Christendom, with the See of Peter".

REFERENCES

1 Geoffrey Goddard, Ninety Years of Ransoming n.d.
2 Martin Gillett, Shrines of Our Lady in England and Wales (1957) p.174
3 King's Lynn Advertiser 27 August 1897 in Walsingham: 100 Years of Pilgrimage 1897-1997 compiled by T. V. McDonald, p.25; Report in Eastern Daily Press quoted in Claude Fisher, Walsingham A Place of Pilgrimage for All People (1983) p.180
4 Gillett, op cit., p.176f
5 Walsingham: 100 Years of Pilgrimage 1897-1997, p.50
6 Eastern Daily Press 20 August 1934; Times 13 April 1936; M. Gillett, op. cit., p.317
7 Gillett, op. cit., p.317f.; Times 4 July 1938, in Walsingham: 100 Years of Pilgrimage 1897-1997, p.60f
8 Times 13 April 1936 Walsingham: 100 Years of Pilgrimage 1897-1997 p.54, Fisher, op. cit., p.91
9 A. Bond and C. Fisher, The Story of Our Lady of Walsingham, (1950), p.7
10 Archaeological Journal Vol. 13 (1856) p.114-133
11 E. R. James, Notes on the Pilgrim Way in West Sussex (1877); J. J. Jusserand English Wayfaring Life in the Middle Ages (1889); J. Cartwright, The Pilgrim's Way from Winchester to Canterbury (1893); Hilaire Belloc The Old Road (1904); A. T. Quiller-Couch The Pilgrim's Way. A Little Scrip of Good Counsel for Travellers. (1906).
12 J. G. Davies, Pilgrimage Yesterday and Today (1988) p.152-8
13 Horace Keast, Our Lady in England (1984) chapters 9-12; Donald Hole Walsingham, England's Nazareth 3rd ed. (1985), p. 31; Richard K. Cowie, The League of Our Lady in Ave (the paper of the Society of Mary) New Series No. 9 (1948)
14 Our Lady of Walsingham. A Review 1921-1928. 'The honour, to a very large extent, of the revival of these pilgrimages rests with the officials of the League of

Our Lady, who dared to make the great adventure when others stood aloof'

15 Robert Farmer, The Catholic League 1913-1988
16 Colin Stephenson, Walsingham Way (1970) chapter 8 passim, p.194-200
17 Colin Stephenson, op. cit. p.144
18 Walsingham edited by Peter G. Cobb (1990), p.8f, p.66
19 Walsingham edited by Peter G. Cobb (1990), p.67f
20 Our Lady's Mirror (the quarterly paper of the Society of Our Lady of Walsingham) Summer 1927; Dereham and Fakenham Times June 1927
21 Our Lady's Mirror July 1926
22 Our Lady's Mirror Autumn 1932, Autumn 1935, Autumn 1936
23 Our Lady's Mirror Summer 1938
24 Our Lady's Mirror Summer 1939
25 Our Lady's Mirror Winter 1939
26 Our Lady's Mirror Winter 1943
27 A. Bond and C. Fisher op. cit., p.7; C. D. Smith A Pocket Guide to Walsingham (1988) p.16
28 Our Lady's Mirror Autumn 1945
29 Walsingham: 100 Years of Pilgrimage 1897-1997, p. 62-69; M. Gillett, op. cit., p.321; A. Bond and C. Fisher, op. cit., p.8; C. Fisher, op. cit., p.45
30 Daily Telegraph 16 August 1954, in Walsingham: 100 Years of Pilgrimage 1897-1997, p.72f; M. Gillett, op. cit., p.322f; C. Fisher, op. cit., p.116
31 C. Fisher, op. cit., p.65
32 The Walsingham Review (successor to Our Lady's Mirror), 13, 43
33 Our Lady's Mirror Winter 1955, Spring 1956, Winter/Spring 1957
34 The Walsingham Review, 87
35 The Walsingham Review, 101
36 The Walsingham Review, 20, 23
37 Walsingham: 100 Years of Pilgrimage 1897-1997, p.93-98
38 Walsingham: 100 Years of Pilgrimage 1897-1997, p.115
39 C. Fisher, op. cit., p.55f, p.84f, p.88; Walsingham: 100 Years of Pilgrimage 1897-1997, p. 89
40 John Bryden Behold the Wood. A History of the Student Cross Pilgrimage 1948-1998, (1998) chapter 8
41 The Walsingham Review, 37; P. G. Cobb Walsingham, p. 85
42 C. Fisher, op. cit., p68f
43 Walsingham: 100 Years of Pilgrimage 1897-1997, p.101
44 H. R. T. Brandreth, The Oecumenical Ideals of the Oxford Movement (1947)
45 Our Lady's Mirror Summer 1934